FRIEDLÆNDER

FROM VAN EYCK TO BRUEGEL

VOLUME ONE

MAX J. FRIEDLÆNDER

FROM VAN EYCK TO BRUEGEL

EDITED AND ANNOTATED

BY F. GROSSMANN

VOLUME ONE

THE FIFTEENTH CENTURY

PHAIDON

ALL RIGHTS RESERVED BY PHAIDON PRESS LTD
5 CROMWELL PLACE · LONDON SW7

FIRST PUBLISHED 1956
SECOND EDITION 1965
THIRD EDITION 1969

PHAIDON PUBLISHERS INC · NEW YORK
DISTRIBUTORS IN THE UNITED STATES: FREDERICK A. PRAEGER · INC
111 FOURTH AVENUE · NEW YORK · N.Y. 10003
LIBRARY OF CONGRESS CATALOG CARD NUMBER: 69–19803

Translated from the German
by Marguerite Kay

Cased (in one volume)
SBN 7148 1375 3
Paperback (in two volumes)
SBN 7148 1377 X (Volume 1)
SBN 7148 1378 8 (Volume 2)

MADE IN GREAT BRITAIN
TEXT PRINTED BY HAZELL WATSON & VINEY LTD · AYLESBURY
COLOUR PLATES PRINTED BY HUNT BARNARD & CO. LTD · AYLESBURY
MONOCHROME PLATES PRINTED BY CAVENDISH PRESS LTD · LEICESTER

CONTENTS

NOTE

Friedländer's *Von Eyck bis Bruegel* was first published in German in 1916 and a second, enlarged edition appeared in 1921.

The first English edition was published by the Phaidon Press in 1956, in the author's ninetieth year. It contained over three hundred illustrations, and was reprinted with corrections in 1964. This third English edition is issued in paperback as well as in cloth. The paperback edition has been divided into two self-contained volumes, the first covering the fifteenth century and the second covering the sixteenth century.

FOREWORD

Written some forty years ago, Friedländer's *Von Eyck bis Bruegel* is one of the few art-historical books of its period which have lost nothing of their impact since they were first published. We value it as the mature work of the unrivalled connoisseur and historian of early Netherlandish painting who, in his fiftieth year, here presented a series of artists' portraits, the fruits, without the labour, of his continuous detailed studies and intuitive insight. What is summed up here in concise, often epigrammatic form in a single tome was later expanded by the author in the fourteen volumes of his magnum opus, *Die Altniederländische Malerei*, published 1924–1937. In this later publication he was able to devote more space to the discussion also of minor artists and to the elaboration of detail which he had avoided in *Von Eyck bis Bruegel*, and, of course, his continuous searching study of the subject, as well as the appearance of hitherto unknown material—paintings and documents—necessarily led to some new results. It is a measure of the earlier work's high quality that in spite of subsequent writings and Friedländer's still continuing work it has in no way become obsolete. The reasons are obvious: in 1916, when he was writing it, his notion of early Netherlandish art was fully developed and formed, and he was complete master of a unique style of expressive characterization which in its elegance and precision and absence of art-historical jargon has few equals in German academic writing.

The first German edition appeared in 1916, a second enlarged one in 1921. It is on the latter that this first English edition, published in the author's ninetieth year, is based.

In the republication of a book of this order any interference with the text is out of the question and the editor's task is a very limited one. In annotating the volume I have tried to enhance its usefulness for the present-day reader mainly in three ways: by indicating changes in the ownership of works discussed, by drawing attention to later relevant discoveries, in particular those of Friedländer himself, and by pointing out, wherever necessary, his most recent views. In order to leave the text completely unchanged, all this matter appears in footnotes which are marked with an asterisk to distinguish them from the author's own. The lists of paintings to be found in the original German edition have been omitted, as Friedländer has provided more extensive ones in *Die Altniederländische Malerei*.

As regards the illustrations, the publishers have generously accepted many of my suggestions and have greatly expanded the original number. Here our aim has been a threefold one: to show the paintings on which Friedländer's main arguments are based, to add to these some typical examples of each artist's work (including some pictures which, discovered later and mostly published by Friedländer himself, have confirmed his original ideas) and finally to provide a supplement which in itself may serve as a pictorial survey of early Netherlandish art.

I have to thank all those who have helped by supplying the photographs and permitting their reproduction and by providing information about the present whereabouts of a number of paintings. While my greatest debt here is to Dr. H. Gerson and the Rijksbureau voor kunsthistorische Documentatie at The Hague and to Mr. Peter Murray and the Witt Library in London, I am no less grateful for the replies to my inquiries received from Mr. E. Haverkamp Begemann, Professor J. G. van Gelder, Dr. Hans Konrad Röthel, Dr. Alfred Scharf, Dr. A. B. de Vries and Professor Ellis K. Waterhouse.

London, 1956   F. Grossmann

NOTE TO THE SECOND EDITION

The 1956 edition of this book was to be the last publication of a major work of Max J. Friedländer in his life-time. He died in Amsterdam on October 11, 1958, in his 92nd year. Almost to the end he remained active, and among the papers he left there was a book, practically completed, on Lucas van Leyden (his third detailed study of the artist), to which Friedrich Winkler had very little to add when he edited it for posthumous publication in 1963. The style and the method of approach to the artist's work are the same, and of the same vigour, in this late book as in his early classic opus *From van Eyck to Bruegel*, which, with very slight changes only, is here reprinted from the 1956 edition.

In the present edition Friedländer's text has, of course, again remained un-altered. The notes, too, have been left unchanged though in a few cases they have been expanded by references to facts which have come to light in the last years. In addition recent changes of ownership have been indicated. Finally, it is my pleasant duty to thank Professor Egbert Haverkamp Begemann for further valuable information and Dr. Michael Kauffmann for help in checking some dates.

Manchester, 1964   F. G.

NOTE TO THE THIRD EDITION

On the whole the principles of annotation and revision have remained the same as in the previous edition. The annotation has, however, been somewhat expanded in order to add to a classic text the usefulness of a reference book.

University of Washington, Seattle, 1969   F. G.

INTRODUCTION

What the reader will find in my essays is an endeavour to put into words the characteristic qualities of various painters. At the same time he will be given the fragmentary results of a student's experience of attribution problems which, though often ridiculed, nevertheless seems to me if not the purpose at least the basis for any serious art research, and in which those gentlemen who look haughtily down on it also participate—though generally with little talent.

I must warn the reader against the mistaken notion that it is possible to recognize the work of a particular painter through implicit faith in a formulated characterization. Failure to do so does not necessarily discredit or refute the characterization. I myself never use fixed ideas of my impressions as a means of attribution and harbour grave misgivings against all persons who use quotations to establish, attack or defend attributions.

Correct attributions generally appear spontaneously and 'prima vista'. We recognize a friend without ever having determined wherein his particular qualities lie and that with a certainty that not even the most detailed description can give.

Such unthinking recognition may be regarded as unscientific whilst the 'method' that Giovanni Morelli imagined, or asserted, that he had found may be admired as scientific. I am convinced that Morelli for all his method would have achieved nothing had he not been a talented connoisseur, more, I am convinced that he never used his method but that he shrouded the results of intuitive connoisseurship in a mantle of false erudition to make them appear unassailable to the naive mind.

Attributions cannot be proved or disproved. And mistakes are only recognized as mistakes when they wither and die. Here the only criterion for truth is that it should prove fruitful. A correct attribution evokes further attributions, a false one, even if it is armed to the teeth with powerful arguments, cannot endure and in due course will prove null and void.

Scientifically speaking, we can regard every discovery of style analysis as a hypothesis and erect airy structures with the intuitively discovered data, confident that documents and signatures, to which we aspire with the help of the provisional structure, will later give a greater solidity to the whole.

Unlike the copper-plate in engraving, the creative personality does not produce commensurably equal works. Therefore it is the problematic task of the connoisseur to perceive in the one production the productive power as a whole with all its potentialities, so that any further work will be recognized as a result of this particular power.

Various things can be deduced from such a concept. There is little advantage in recording and learning by heart all the characteristics of a work of art, because it is not in the least likely that all of them will recur in a second work. We must distinguish between what is necessary for the author and what is accidental—and only effective in the one case—such as size and subject-matter. It is not advisable to scrutinize too intently. It is a good thing to examine in rapid sequence as many works by a master as are accessible, and then to gather and assimilate the impressions away from the monuments. This is the best way to harmonize the versatility of the critic with the potential abilities of the creative personality.

My essays cannot serve directly as a guide to connoisseurship, and could not do so even if they were more successful and detailed in the characterization. Indirectly—and this is the extent of the modest hope that sustains me—they may facilitate and intensify the study and the enjoyment of the originals. The ability to attribute and check attributions will then follow automatically from study and enjoyment. Yes, from enjoyment!

Many art historians, it is true, make it their ambition to exclude pleasure from art, in which, for obvious reasons, some of them succeed all too well. They are embarrassed and afraid that representatives of the more strictly disciplined sister sciences will not regard them as equals but will suspect them of an entertaining or frivolous occupation. Reasoning based on calculations and measurements is presented as the true method. A dry approach stands high in favour. Abstruseness, involved terminology, which makes the reading of art-historical books such torture, derives from that very ambition. Sometimes there are depths, but so obscure as to be worthless for the reader, generally all is shallow but cunningly troubled so as to suggest depths.

It can never be the aim of a science to ignore the specific and essential quality of its subject—and the specific and essential quality of art is the impression it makes. I do not know what organs would remain with which to apprehend a work of art once enjoyment had been sacrificed to the ideal of ascetic, scientific method.

Aphoristic remarks, put together unsystematically, are best suited to transmit pictorial impressions, to spotlight particular characteristics. I do not believe that a more detailed and fuller description, which would be full of wearying repetitions, could serve the purpose better. Strictest economy of words seems advisable since the receptive power of the reader must be regarded as limited. No reader is able to retain endless descriptions of form and colour.

FROM VAN EYCK TO BRUEGEL

THE FIFTEENTH CENTURY

THE GEOGRAPHY

OF NETHERLANDISH ART

WHEN we speak of Flemish and Dutch painting we mean the entire area—so rich in art during the fifteenth and seventeenth centuries—lying within the political boundaries of Belgium and the Kingdom of the Netherlands. The contrast between Dutch and Flemish is especially clear in the painting of the seventeenth century and a comparison between the personalities of Rubens and Rembrandt imprints it firmly on our minds.

In the fifteenth century the dividing line is not equally clear. The political and religious differences were formed, or at least intensified, by the long wars of independence against the clerical and feudal domination of Spain. As a final result of these wars the Northern states, that is substantially the modern Kingdom of the Netherlands, became a self-contained Protestant community whilst the Southern provinces, that is substantially modern Belgium, remained orthodox and under Habsburg rule. In the South the doors were wide open to the influx of Latin culture; the North shut itself off with puritanical strictness and preserved its Germanic culture intact. In the fifteenth century the Netherlands were more of an entity with a uniform culture and the Germanic essence, blended it is true with Latin elements from France and Burgundy, flowed through the entire land. In their critical study of painting scholars have attempted, with some success, to discern even in the fifteenth century the contrast that was later to become so evident, but the scarcity of monuments in present-day Holland—a result of the iconoclasm of the sixteenth century—is a serious handicap.

To apply the term 'Flemish' to the Habsburg states in the South is not correct and posits a part for the whole. Strictly speaking this geographical concept embraces only the two counties of Flanders but leaves out Hainaut, Liège, Brabant and other parts which had a greater share in the art life of the non-Dutch Netherlands than had Flanders. It would be better to expand the concept Flemish, not incorrectly, and speak of the

Southern Netherlands, modern Belgium, as opposed to the Northern Netherlands, modern Holland.

The artistic predominance of the Flemish provinces is a mere illusion. Bruges and Ghent in the fifteenth, Antwerp in the sixteenth century were flourishing commercial centres with an international prosperous mercantile society which attracted artistic talent. In addition to the Burgundian princes, who were of real importance as patrons of artists and introduced the exacting demands of the French court, we note with some surprise a comparatively large number of Italian merchants as patrons (Tommaso Portinari, Jacopo Tani, Giovanni Arnolfini and others). In the sixteenth century the export of art works to Spain assumed vast dimensions and Spanish demands determined the work in the Antwerp workshops. A study of Dürer's Netherlandish diary gives a good idea of the international character of the upper strata of the Antwerp population.

If then what we might call the consumers were by no means pure Flemish, the producers were still less so. Of the masters who set the course for Bruges art hardly one was of Flemish origin. Jan van Eyck came from Maaseyck, a place on the Meuse north of Maestricht, where the political boundaries of Belgium, Germany and Holland meet. The area around Maaseyck should be kept in mind as a central source for Netherlandish art. Hans Memlinc came from Germany, presumably from Mömlingen on the Middle Rhine,[1] Gerard David from Oudewater, which lies in Holland between Gouda and Utrecht. Jan Provost was a native of Mons, that is to say from Hainaut in the South, Ambrosius Benson from Milan. With the exception of Hugo van der Goes and Justus van Gent who may have come from the Flemish city of Ghent, no important painter of the fifteenth century, and very few of the sixteenth, can with any probability be traced to Flanders.

Round about 1500 Antwerp became the artistic reservoir and melting pot. Painters gathered there from every province in the Netherlands. Of the celebrities who determined the character of the art of Antwerp with its flourishing export, Quentin Massys had immigrated from Louvain (Brabant), Jan Gossaert from Maubeuge (Hainaut), the Master of the Death of the Virgin is probably identical with Joos who came from Cleves. Large numbers of unknown artists are entered in the surviving Antwerp guild lists and in many cases the names, though they tell us nothing else, at least show the place of origin. The North (Holland) and

*[1] Cf. p. 41 note 1.

the East (Northern Brabant and Limburg) seem to have been particularly rich in artistic talent. Roughly speaking the situation may be summed up as follows: the flourishing commercial cities, Bruges in the fifteenth century, later Antwerp, were comparatively poor in artistic talent but attracted artists from all parts of the Netherlands, particularly from the East. If we draw a circle with Antwerp as centre and Antwerp-Maaseyck as radius the circumference line runs roughly through the places of origin of the painters whose influence was decisive, namely Tournai (Rogier van der Weyden and Robert Campin, who is presumably identical with the Master of Flémalle), Mons (Provost), Maubeuge (Gossaert), Dinant (Patenier), Hertogenbosch (Jerome Bosch), Oudewater (Gerard David).

Any consideration of Netherlandish art from the racial angle must be largely determined by linguistic boundaries and, moreover, conclusions necessarily drawn from modern conditions are bound to be of doubtful validity for the fifteenth and sixteenth centuries. The Flemish cities which were presumably entirely Germanic in the fifteenth century can, according to my interpretation, be left entirely out of account.

Holland, the influence of which in the structure of South Netherlandish art was demonstrably strong, may be regarded as a Germanic area. The area of Northern Brabant (Hertogenbosch, Limburg, Maaseyck) must be described as predominantly German in the wider sense, so that not only Geertgen, Jan Mostaert, Lucas van Leyden, Jacob van Amsterdam but also Jerome Bosch and Pieter Bruegel of the later artists, and Pol de Limburg and his brother—outstanding book illuminators in the service of French princes at the end of the fourteenth century—and the brothers Hubert and Jan van Eyck may be accepted with some degree of probability as painters of Germanic extraction. On the other hand the racial origin of the artists who came to Brabant and Flanders from the South seems problematical, namely the painters who were born at Tournai, Mons, Maubeuge, Dinant.

How to classify the Master of Flémalle and Rogier van der Weyden is a particularly important question. According to recent research the Master of Flémalle seems rather older than Rogier, almost a contemporary of Jan van Eyck, and his genius is regarded as at least equal to that of Rogier, though, admittedly, in his types and compositional motifs Rogier obviously exerted a stronger and wider influence than any other painter of the fifteenth century. It is now assumed on very plausible grounds that the Master of Flémalle is identical with the Robert Campin who is documented as teacher of Rogier at Tournai. If this is correct then the two masters represent an art that was native in Tournai, the peculiarities of which, especially in their contrast to Eyckian art, are more pronounced in Rogier than in the Master of Flémalle.

Tournai lies in the French-speaking zone. There is, I am afraid, no satisfactory scientific method of determining Rogier's racial derivation but it would be tempting to regard the contrast between Jan van Eyck, who came from the East, and Rogier, who came from the South, as a conflict between the German and the Latin temperament with the towns of Flanders providing the battleground. Round about 1450 the battle seems to be going in Rogier's favour.

It is not hard to recognize the far-reaching difference between Jan van Eyck and Rogier, but it would be imprudent to regard the two personalities as representative of their respective races. At any rate the utmost caution should be exercised. If we possessed a greater number of both French and Dutch, i.e. Germanic-Netherlandish, paintings of the fifteenth century, a careful check-up might prove fruitful. We could then contrast what the Dutch and the Van Eycks have in common on the one hand with what the masters of Tournai and the French have on the other. Unfortunately we possess very few purely Dutch and still fewer French paintings so that the examination of a rich and varied material becomes impossible.

The genius of Jan van Eyck certainly transcends purely racial qualities whilst the fanatically bitter spirituality of Rogier seems more individually than racially determined. But to a certain degree only. And it is in the estimation of this degree that the almost insoluble difficulty lies.

Essential for Jan van Eyck's art is the positive pleasure, the indiscriminate unprejudiced delight in the appearance of things. The illusion itself is the goal, reached in a blaze of triumph. He accepts the whole of the visible world without any preferences. Searching observation and a persistent study of the model suppress subjective invention and sweep tradition aside.

Compared with Jan van Eyck, Rogier seems immaterial and intellectual. The subject-matter dominates him from the outset and he works under the spell of traditional pattern but his mind is rich in imagery. He looks at nature with a selective eye and never follows her call down unknown paths to adventure. Pure in style, with a surely controlled austerity of expression that befits the devotional picture, his art appears poor and monotonous compared with Jan van Eyck's art, which finds constant renewal in the infinite richness of nature. Jan van Eyck is an explorer (Rogier is an inventor). He perceives air, light and chiaroscuro and how things are related in space. Rogier composes like a sculptor, a carver in relief, by isolating the figure groups in his mind and adding the landscape backgrounds; he disposes the plastically conceived figures on the surface like a draughtsman by emphasizing the contours, Jan van Eyck conceives and represents as a painter. Beside Rogier's elaborately constructed compositions Eyck's works have the accidental charm of the picturesque, the pulsating warmth and individual richness of life itself. By the impetus of his thrust Jan van Eyck is carried further towards his own goal than any other painter of the fifteenth century. Taking the contrast between Eyck and Rogier as a touchstone for the evaluation of the other known Netherlandish painters, Geertgen tot Sint Jans of Haarlem, who represents the purely Dutch art, stands closer to Eyck than to Rogier.

Apart from personal genius that triumphantly transcends place and time, we may regard as Germanic heritage the impulse to observe nature that bears such fruit throughout Eyck's work and confers a universally acknowledged superiority on Netherlandish panel painting. Rogier's constructive form, and clear-cut pictorial ideas, which for two generations supplied Netherlandish workshops and painters far beyond the boundaries of the land with a formalized pattern of expression, can be regarded as half French. For is not the contrast between Claude and Ruysdael, between Watteau and Gainsborough, too, in some measure the contrast between the constructive draughtsman and the observant painter? France's supreme achievement in religious architecture and in the grand sculpture of the Middle Ages went far beyond what was achieved in the Germanic lands. An additional symptom of the innate French genius for architecture and sculpture.

The Southern Netherlands, especially the cities of Flanders and Brabant that flourished in the fifteenth and sixteenth centuries, draw their artistic talent from the half-French South and the Germanic East. The North Netherlandish, Dutch art may be regarded as purely Germanic, whereas in Flanders and Brabant Eyckian observation blends with the formalism of Rogier, the German with the Latin.

JAN VAN EYCK

HISTORY checks the flow of events and bestows a false importance on certain personalities by calling them founders and inaugurators. We do not do otherwise—even though our conscience may be more troubled—than did Carel van Mander, a Netherlandish painter who around 1600 zealously collected information from traditional sources on the painters of his country. This chronicler begins the history of Netherlandish painting, or at least his series of vitae, with the Van Eycks, just as we begin the history of the printed book with Gutenberg.

Naturally there were painters in the Netherlands before the van Eycks. Naturally the van Eycks were sons as well as fathers. Van Mander's idea was mistaken but it was a mistake in which was expressed a tradition that was widespread around 1600. The painters of the sixteenth century venerated the van Eycks as ancestors and founders of their craft. In the North they were the first to emerge with a personal achievement from the 'dark' Middle Ages with their anonymous craftsmanship. Only the creative power of genius could bequeath a memory that was woven into the Eyck legend, the Eyck cult.

We should argue along these lines even if nothing had survived of the brothers' work. But the vivid impression of the existing monuments blends with the venerable tradition. With the van Eycks a source of power seems to erupt from the ground. Nothing comes out of nothing. But what goes on underground is hidden from our eyes. Here if anywhere the mistaken idea of a beginning is excusable and is indispensable for the historian.

Jan van Eyck, the younger brother, is supposed to have invented something, namely oil painting—for the Netherlanders of the sixteenth century this meant quite simply painting. It was thought that quotations of old painter recipes, long before the van Eycks, in which oil is mentioned, could do away with this tradition. Jan van Eyck's painting technique differed from that of his predecessors. But the chronicler naively confuses cause and effect. The invention did not come first. Jan van Eyck—or Hubert van Eyck—was not able to paint as he painted after and because he had invented the technique of oil, rather is it true that he found new media because the urge to paint as he painted could not be satisfied with the media hitherto in use. His search for new processes was stimulated and guided by observation, imagination and creative will.

Even though the age and the people had their share in this innovation, the inborn love of heroes could have found expression here had not two personalities instead of one laid claim to the honour of the one achievement, namely Hubert and Jan. If genius is rare then the law of averages makes us quite incredulous at the tidings that one pair of parents could produce two geniuses as sons. Wherever two brothers combine for one creative task we suspect from the very outset that one of them is a subordinate assistant. The happy collaboration of craftsmen is conceivable but the way of genius is to command or to repel. Again and again this persistent prejudice has urged historians to make a clean sweep once and for all of the legend of the two founders of Netherlandish painting.

The Ghent altarpiece bears an inscription which reads in English: 1–10
"The painter Hubert van Eyck who was surpassed by none (*maior quo nemo repertus*) began the work. Johannes, second in the art, completed it at the request of Jodocus Vyd in the year 1432 on the 16th of May." This text, which is not everywhere fully intact, poses almost as many problems as it answers.

Should the order of precedence of the brothers be simply accepted? Should it be regarded as a pious lie or a modest piece of self-deception on the part of the younger brother, who was responsible for the inscription? It remains probable that Hubert undertook the Ghent altarpiece which, about the year 1420, was designed to surpass all other altar decorations in the Netherlands in size and richness of content. If nothing had survived but the Ghent altarpiece we would accept without question the order of precedence of the inscription and regard Jan van Eyck as the collaborator, pupil and imitator of his elder brother. But apart from the Ghent altarpiece works by Jan have survived, done by him alone, after the death of Hubert (1426), works unequivocally signed with his name, devotional panels and portraits such as the van der Paele altar panel of 1436 and the *Arnolfini Couple* of 1434. In view of these works by Jan it   16, 20 becomes difficult to uphold the order of precedence of the Ghent inscription. There means and end seem in perfect harmony. The instrument is handled as only he can handle it who has made it for himself. Could such skill really be inherited and not acquired?

The scales are almost equally balanced. On Hubert's side in addition to his being the first-born is the superlative of the Ghent inscription; on Jan's side is the ever renewed impact of his pictures and, though this carries less weight, his fame in olden times—Hubert's name was almost forgotten.

Critics approached the Ghent altarpiece confidently, convinced that stylistic analysis could solve all problems. The composite altarpiece, however, gave a different answer to each observer.

Every conceivable argument has been used to separate Hubert's share from that of Jan. It would be waste of time to compare the results. Dvořák's division[1] is the only solution which, if not correct, is at least satisfying in principle. The representatives of two generations, of two phases of art, are revealed in the Ghent altarpiece, or, if this aim is not achieved, at least the trend of the analysis is significant. Hubert's personality takes shape in the thoughtful and detailed study of the Vienna scholar as a master of the older generation who executed in what we can see today the three main figures of the upper row and some half of the central panel below. Dvořák attempts to show that these parts are conceived in a fundamentally different manner from the rest, that they had no part in the specifically Eyckian achievement. It was Jan who took the decisive step. Consistently, Dvořák claims all Eyckian paintings, even the unsigned ones, apart from the Ghent altarpiece, for Jan. In this interpretation Hubert's personality goes under, submerged in the general anonymity of pre-Eyckian craftsmanship.

Dvořák's interpretation has not been generally accepted. Over and again attempts have been made to place Hubert next to Jan as a personality of equal importance. Even the idea that Jan's art, like the moon, shines only with reflected light, the afterglow of Hubert's art, even this idea persists.

Jan's accredited works together with the information about him gleaned from archives give a tolerably well-defined picture. We first hear of him in the service of Count John of Holland (1422) and, immediately after that patron's death, of Philip of Burgundy. The warlike and splendour-loving rulers of those days restricted their luxury and their love of art to easily transportable things, to rich materials, jewels and books. For camp and tent life they favoured a maximum of art in a minimum of bulk and weight. The concentrated preciosity of Eyckian art was certainly calculated to satisfy this desire.

In a letter of the year 1524 we find the following revealing passage: *gran maestro Joannes che prima fe l'arte d' illuminare libri sive ut hodie loquimur miniare. . . .* According to this Jan began by doing book illuminations, had therefore probably been trained in a book illuminator's

---

[1] Vienna *Jahrbuch*, vol. XXIV.

workshop. Did the master's art evolve from older book illumination and is that the reason for its contrast to the panel painting of his own generation? The theory finds support from more than one side. Viewed in its relationship to the book illumination that had developed on French soil around 1400 (with, so it would seem, the decisive participation of Netherlandish artists) Jan's art, though it loses none of its brilliance, originality or historical importance, does lose some of its inexplicability.

Until 1902 Eyckian miniatures were only dreamed of. Then the unexpected that might have been expected actually happened: Eyckian miniatures came to light. Art criticism reacted as it always does on such 22, 23 occasions, turned a deaf ear, refused to accept the new. In 1902 Durrieux published *Les heures de Turin*, a fragment of a prayer book, on which quite obviously various hands had worked at different times, and in which several pages have an Eyckian flavour. Two years later this prayer book fell a victim to the flames. This, the most serious loss sustained in recent times in the world of art, is slightly mitigated by three circumstances. In the first place, immediately before its destruction, the book attracted attention and was published in reasonably good collotype. Secondly Georges Hulin, the keenly discerning critic of early Netherlandish painting, examined the pages thoroughly, found in them the key to the solution of all Eyckian problems and set down the results of his examination. Finally a second fragment of the prayer book turned up at Milan in the Trivulziana[1] and in this part too there are pages of an Eyckian character.

One page of the Turin fragment represents Duke William of Bavaria on horseback with his retinue on the shores of the North Sea, offering up a prayer to heaven. The prayer book was owned by this duke sometime between 1414 and 1417, the year of his death. The miniature is thus dated, excitingly early, considerably earlier than any other known work by the van Eycks. Several more pages at Turin and Milan are certainly by the same hand of approximately the same date (the book contains in addition considerably older and appreciably younger work). That the Eyckian style should have been imitated by about 1417 in a book illuminator's workshop seems in itself highly improbable and in addition, the freshness, freedom and boldness of the illuminations (even in the poor reproductions) compel us to attribute them to the founder of Netherlandish painting. Particularly in the landscape painting, in the observation of light and in the mood, the miniatures, limited as they are in size, surpass everything else we have of the van Eycks. The art revealed here

*1 This part is now in the Museo Civico, Turin.

does not by any means differ from the art of the panel paintings in the sense that it is inferior or derived. Even those art critics who do reckon with the possibility of change generally forget to reckon with its necessity. Jan van Eyck must have painted otherwise in 1417 than in 1427.

The master of 1417, whoever he may have been, began the conquest of the visible world in landscape, rendering it with unparalleled illusion not only in the structure but also in the conditions of light, and endowing it with permanent validity. The local colours are adjusted to the dominant tone with inexplicable confidence. The gliding of shadows, the rippling of waves, the reflection in the water, cloud formations: all that is most evanescent and most delicate is expressed with easy mastery. A realism that the entire century failed to reach seems to have been achieved once by the impetus of the first attack.

The figures, in strange contrast to such freedom in the landscape, are closely linked to the Gothic tradition, little individualized, with flowing garments and of uncertain construction.

Hulin (in his publication *Les heures de Milan*) believed that he had discovered in the prayer book something more than the Eyckian style of 1417. It seemed to him, that the personalities of Hubert and Jan emerge here more distinctly than in the Ghent altarpiece.

In addition to the admirable pages in the *Turin-Milan prayer book* there are a few others, that deviate in style, which also have an Eyckian character, but Eyckian in a different sense, matter-of-fact in the landscape with no atmospheric charm and with stiff, straight drapery folds. Not a single page of this second group can be dated. If, as Hulin assumes, both groups originated around 1417 then the old problem is solved. Hubert— and this is Hulin's momentous conclusion—produced the miniatures of the first group, which appear archaic as a whole, Jan the superficially Eyckian but weaker pages of the second group. That is to say the order of precedence of the Ghent inscription would be confirmed. Hulin did not hesitate to draw the consequences from his division of the miniatures and attributed panels such as the wing panels in St. Petersburg[1] and the 13 Berlin *Madonna in the Church* to the elder brother.

I have never, unfortunately, seen the Turin fragment and hesitate to contradict the Belgian scholar, whose revolutionary proposal is the apparently inevitable result of a study of the miniatures. I cannot, however, suppress some doubts. The weakest point in Hulin's argument is the impossibility of dating the second group. The wide divergence of style between the two brothers around 1417 seems remarkable. Surely at such

*[1] Now in the Metropolitan Museum of Art, New York.

an early date the difference in style should be slight. About 1425—in the Ghent altarpiece—the discrepancy is far smaller and so indistinct that even Hulin does not dare to attempt a separation between the two hands.

I am in complete agreement with Hulin's verdict on the first group and do not consider his praise of these pages in any way exaggerated. He who produced them was the founder of Netherlandish art. And if Hubert is the author then the inscription *maior quo nemo repertus* is true and Jan would be relegated to second place. My opinion of the second group differs from that of Hulin.

These pages are Eyckian but they lack the style characteristics of the early primitive. Their quality is by no means so exceptional that it could not have been attained by a follower of Van Eyck around 1440 (at this late date work was still being done on the prayer book). If by such a valuation the second group is set aside then the way becomes free— contrary to Hulin's view—to install Jan as the author of the first group. This change certainly has some advantages. In 1422 Jan was in the service of John of Bavaria; all the more probable that he had previously been associated with John's brother William of Bavaria, whereas there is no record of a connection between Hubert and any royal personage. In olden times Jan (not Hubert) was spoken of as a book illuminator.

The attempt to obtain an over-all picture of Jan's art, to trace a line of development with some degree of probability by including the miniatures in his *oeuvre* leads to a tolerably satisfying result. Those panel paintings that a few experts have always regarded as particularly early works by Jan, such as the *Crucifixion* in Berlin, the *Three Maries at the Sepulchre* in the Cook collection, Richmond,[1] and the wing panels in St. Petersburg, 11 are closest to the miniatures, the panels produced after the Ghent altarpiece are furthest away. The line of development can be drawn through the Ghent altarpiece. If a corresponding attempt is made to draw a line from Hulin's second group to the late signed panels of Jan then the result, it seems to me, is less satisfying.

I am well aware that my reconstruction is one which, though it yields a full picture of Jan's art, has, in addition to other weaknesses, the disadvantage of leaving Hubert's personality in the obscurity to which Dvořák banished it.

In their colour effect Jan van Eyck's pictures show the same characteristics that first strike one in Rembrandt's paintings: they are dark without being black. They are brunette, warm, golden, a darkness that glows with colour. They have the inner brilliance of a precious jewel-like

*[1] Now in the Museum Boymans-Van Beuningen, Rotterdam.

substance. Certain materials such as brittle, scaly, splintered rock, downy feathers, hair, and fur, creased silk or the shining gleam of armour, are set off with all the delight of a discoverer. The discerning drawing that searches out the detail never becomes laborious. A soft colour harmony encompasses and unites the steely sharpness of the formal design. The linear framework of the flesh is built up with folds, furrows and incisions full of brooding darkness. The internal drawing is rich in detail. The outer contour on the other hand is often lightly blurred with shimmering colour, whereas the painters of the fifteenth century normally define essentials in sharply etched outline.

Realism and illusion are all the more exciting at this stage because they are not consistently applied to the whole and to all the parts. Particularly in the works of Jan that I regard as early, but also, though less obviously, in his latest works, the basic conditions of realistic expression remain unfulfilled in the linear perspective and in the proportions of the figures to the surrounding space, conditions that in a later generation were fulfilled even by bunglers. The unity of lighting is an achievement of genius, centuries in advance of the time, but Jan never masters linear perspective. Conventions of form which derive from Gothic tradition, especially in the drapery and the female heads, are in sharp contrast to miracles of individual realism.

In the picture that bears the strange inscription *Johannes de Eyck fuit hic 1434*[1] one of the treasures of the National Gallery, London, a problem has been solved that no painter of the fifteenth century dared to set himself again—that of placing two people, in full-length figure, side by side in a richly appointed room, the Lucchese merchant Giovanni Arnolfini and his wife. A glorious example of the sovereign power of genius! The figures are a little too large but they stand freely in space and air in the shadowy room, for every nuance of colour has been seized with automatic dream-like assurance. The achievement lies in the ability to adapt the complex colour design to a single source of light, to conceive the figures and picture space as a whole, rather than in the careful fashioning of details.

The task was to paint the double portrait of a married couple but it would seem that the master was impelled not only beyond the limits of his theme but also further than the bounds of his own idea. The result surpasses the aim: certainly a sign of creative genius. Every sensitive observer is stimulated to wandering speculation and poetic phantasies.

[*1] The meaning of this strange inscription has been elucidated by Prof. E. Panofsky (in *The Burlington Magazine*, vol. lxiv, 1934, pp. 117 ff.), who regards the painting as a marriage picture and interprets the inscription as "Jan van Eyck was here (as a witness to the marriage)".

We are tempted to interpret the solemn, stiff closeness of the man and the woman in a general, a symbolic way. The 'correct' explanation seems inadequate because it does not do justice to the mood into which the picture plunges us.

Only he who observes superficially is content to admire the amount of formal details and shades of colour that Jan van Eyck has conjured so minutely on to inch-sized surfaces. The more sensitive observer will not fail to note that this work was done in hot-blooded exaltation rather than patiently and with measured skill. Over and beyond this it becomes clear that this passion for appearance, this ferreting out of formal complexities, this respect for the material are born of a new feeling that can be regarded as the herald of a new conception of the world.

The human warmth, the perfect balance of sense and spirit were not transmitted to Jan's successors. As we leave him and turn to other painters of the fifteenth century we pass from the richness of a free, colourful, adventurous and seductive world into a monastery where in the cells hooded men, albeit each in a different way according to his temperament and talent, practise the painter's craft.

PETRUS CHRISTUS

JAN VAN EYCK died in 1441 at Bruges, where he had worked for the greater part of his last decade. In 1444 Petrus Christus became free master at Bruges. He was a native of Baerle, probably the place of that name that lies between Tilburg and Turnhout. As far as our scrappy knowledge goes, this Petrus represents Bruges painting for the period between 1444 and 1472, that is to say for the time between Jan van Eyck's death and the appearance of Memlinc. Bruges art in the second third of the century appears to us as the aftermath of the Eyck tradition, whether Christus was a pupil of Jan or not. Actually there is no lack of indications to suggest that several masters who worked in other parts of the Netherlands, such as the Master of Flémalle, Rogier van der Weyden or Dieric Bouts, intervened in some way in the art of the flourishing commercial city. They came and went but Petrus Christus remained. And his dependence on Jan borders on the parasitical.

A reflection of Eyckian art emanates from everything done by Petrus, endowing the poor achievements with prestige and glamour. His doll-like figures are generally of medium height, they have wide heads in which the temples, foreheads and cheeks seem broad and empty, whilst eyes, mouth and nose are close together. The figures are stuck in wide balloon-like garments with contours that are straight or round and everywhere of little mobility. The large high-set ear is often visible. The hands are short and plump. The sparse hair hangs down in strands.

Especially Eyckian is the small panel in the Berlin Museum with the
30 Virgin and St. Barbara, the so-called *Exeter Madonna*, presented by the same Carthusian friar who presented the Jan van Eyck *Madonna with Two*
15 *Female Saints* belonging to the heirs of Baron Gustave de Rothschild, Paris.[1] Petrus Christus borrowed as much as he needed from the richer composition. His holy women do not rise above the level of pleasant friendliness. It is instructive to compare the stiff outline which divides St. Barbara's hair from her face and the dreary contour that terminates the saint's gown with the expressive drawing of the Eyckian model. Most
31 nearly successful in the Eyckian sense is the portrait of a Monk (the halo is probably a later addition) privately owned at Valencia.[2]

*[1] Now in the Frick Collection, New York.   *[2] Now Metropolitan Museum, New York.

The series of pictures correctly attributed to the master appears firmly defined. The few dates range from 1446 to 1452 (1457?); the undated pictures do not greatly, if at all, exceed these limits. To the generally known works I might add a small *Head of Christ* seen from the front (the signature indistinct) privately owned by Mr. F. Kleinberger, Paris,[1] as well as an *Annunciation* in a private collection, Paris.[2]

His biggest work, the *Lamentation over Christ* in the Brussels Museum, is 27 rather different from his other works and to some extent problematical. Renewed study of the form always confirms the attribution and I am in no doubt as to the authorship. But in order to explain the strange features, a few astonishingly expressive compositional motifs, the richness and the angularity of the drapery, the intervention of some outside source must be assumed which, in addition to Van Eyck's model, or replacing it, affected Petrus Christus.

One figure, the fainting Virgin, is taken from Rogier's *Descent from the* 53 *Cross* in the Escorial.[3] Other figures, such as the rather isolated one of the mourning Mary Magdalen on the left, are as little credible as inventions of the painter as is the obviously borrowed figure of the Virgin. A comparison between the *Lamentation* in Brussels and the one in New York, which lies well within the scope of Petrus Christus's ability and is little 28 more than a schematic version of Eyckian art, enables us to distinguish between the personal and the borrowed elements in the Brussels panel. The dead Christ is similarly placed in both. But his anatomy is much richer in the considerably larger Brussels panel and recalls Dieric Bouts, whose style is also suggested in several of the heads. Since Rogier's Escorial panel was at Louvain, where Bouts lived, a tempting hypothesis is suggested which could explain the turn in Petrus Christus's line of development: The Bruges master might have seen Rogier's altarpiece during a stay at Louvain and at the same time come under the influence of Dieric Bouts. Though, admittedly, the influx into the stagnant waters of Bruges art may have taken place in some other way.

[1] Now in the collection of Mrs. W. R. Timken, New York.
[2] The painting forms part of the Michael Friedsam Bequest to the Metropolitan Museum of Art, New York, where it is now ascribed to "Jan van Eyck and Helpers".
[3] Now in the Prado, Madrid.

ROGIER VAN DER WEYDEN

ROGIER VAN DER WEYDEN and the Master of Flémalle stand very close to one another. How they stand to one another is a question to which various answers have been given. The Master of Flémalle was so to speak created out of a rib of Rogier's by art critics and as soon as he stood tolerably firmly on his own feet he was regarded as a descendant, as a follower of Rogier.

42-43   The only work by the Master of Flémalle which is inscribed with a date, the Werle wings in Madrid, was done in the year 1438. We can scarcely with any certainty ascribe one work by Rogier to so early a date.[1] Judging his personality as a whole, the Flémalle Master seems more archaic than Rogier and like a contemporary of Jan van Eyck.

The youthful Rogier appears closer to the Flémalle Master than does the ageing Rogier. There would be less justification for the assertion: It is just the youthful Master of Flémalle who is close to Rogier. What he could have learnt from Rogier the Master of Flémalle does not possess.

It was tempting to experiment with the hypothesis that the Master of Flémalle was Rogier's teacher. As it happens, the name of this teacher is known. At least there is documentary evidence that a Rogelet de la Pasture was apprenticed to Robert Campin at Tournai in 1426. We know that in 1427 another pupil, Jaquelotte (Jaques) Daret, entered Campin's workshop. This fact provides unexpected support for the assumption that the Master of Flémalle was none other than Robert Campin. Fragments of a work executed in 1434 by Jaques Daret were discovered by George Hulin. Two panels of this altarpiece done for the Abbey St. Vaast at

44-45   Arras, the *Visitation* and the *Adoration of the Kings*, are in the Kaiser-Friedrich Museum, Berlin.[2] Jaques Daret, documented as a pupil of Campin and in the closest sense a fellow-pupil of Rogier's emerges from stylistic criticism as a not particularly firm character and dependent on the Flémalle Master.

We can regard as at least an intelligent working hypothesis the idea that Rogier was a pupil of the Flémalle Master at Tournai. The possibility

*[1] Friedländer later assigned a date earlier than 1438 to the following paintings by Rogier: Diptych with *Virgin and St. Catherine* in Vienna, the *Madonna* from the Northbrook Collection (now at Lugano), the *Portrait of a Woman* in Berlin.
*[2] Now in the Staatliche Museen, Berlin-Dahlem.

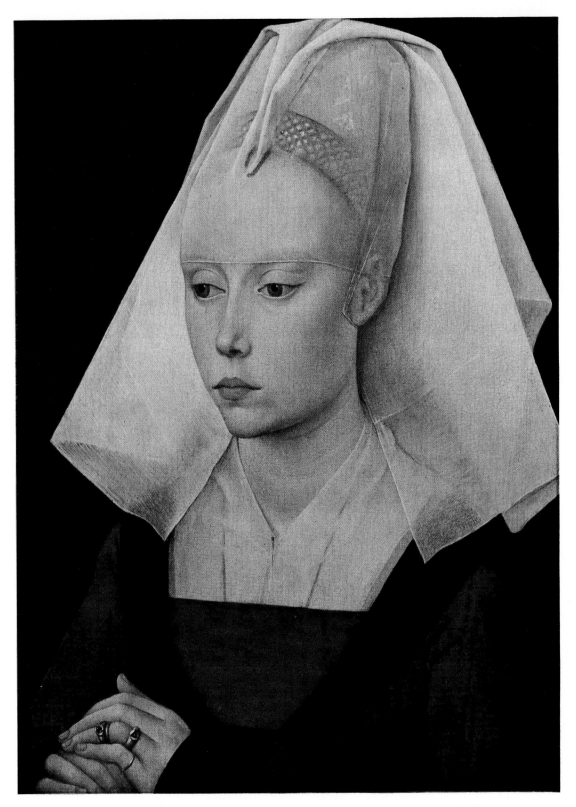

I. Rogier van der Weyden: *Portrait of a Lady*. London, National Gallery

that Rogier as associate and workshop companion also influenced his teacher is the more plausible when we consider that he was not at the customary apprentice age but a man of thirty when he worked with Robert Campin, had possibly already been trained in the paternal sculptor studio,[1] and was by nature strong-willed and dominating.

There is a motif that occurs both on the Werle altarpiece by the Flémalle Master and in Rogier's altarpiece of the *Virgin* so that a borrowing from one side must be assumed. The arm movement and position of the hand of the Saviour appearing to His Mother, in that part 50 of the altarpiece at present owned by Messrs. Duveen,[2] are similar to the arm movement and position of the hand of the Baptist in the donor wing 42 of the Werle altarpiece. As used by Rogier, the movement arises significantly from the situation but not so in the Master of Flémalle's version. The Baptist stands behind the kneeling donor commending and presenting him—a customary motif that is varied here in an unaccustomed way. Movement and gesture of the Baptist are not readily understood. The inference that the Flémalle Master was the borrower has often been drawn. It would be important to fix the terminus ante quem for the altarpiece of the *Virgin*.[3]

There are other ways open to us for dating the altarpiece of the *Virgin* but they are increasingly beset by difficulties. The Berlin gallery has an 49 exact replica of the Granada altarpiece the quality and condition of which has been judged in curiously differing ways; sometimes it is hailed as an original, sometimes rejected as a forgery or as over-painted. Since the Granada version became known, the Berlin replica has been ignored as of no importance. The Berlin altarpiece is unusually well-preserved, it is in some respects inferior to the Granada work but can hardly be other than an extremely careful and highly successful workshop replica.

At Miraflores near Burgos there was, as Ponz recorded in 1793, an altarpiece of the *Virgin* allegedly presented in 1445, the description of which, without a shadow of doubt, fits the work that has survived in two versions. Martin V is said to have presented the altarpiece of Miraflores to King John II. It remains probable that the Berlin altarpiece is identical with the Miraflores one. But if we take the tradition of the presentation seriously then we are forced to assume a suspiciously early date for its

*1 Recent research has established that Rogier's father was not, as had long been believed, the sculptor Henri van der Weyden, but the Tournai master cutler Henry de la Pasture. See also Friedländer himself (in *Die Altniederländische Malerei*, XIV, 1937, p. 81).
*2 Now in the Metropolitan Museum, New York.
*3 Friedländer (in *Die Altniederländische Malerei*, XIV, 1937, p. 84) no longer considered the gesture as of any help for the dating of the New York painting, which he then placed between 1440 and 1445. Cf. also Friedländer, *Die Altniederländische Malerei*, II, 1924, pp. 16 ff.

origin. Rogier was not made free master at Tournai until 1432. For the pope, who died in 1431, to have owned the altarpiece presupposes a reputation of the painter so early as to be hardly credible. At any rate that part of the Ponz report that refers to Martin V is untrustworthy.

Rogier and the Flémalle Master have the kind of relationship that one would expect from a studio association of several years but in character and talent they differ. Each possesses qualities that the other lacks. The Flémalle Master works less purposefully, less comprehensively, unevenly, unpredictable in success as in failure. With a more sensitive eye for the surface, the skin of things, for light, air and colour, he is less interested in construction than Rogier. He proceeds from observation, Rogier from the idea. He approaches us with human and sensuous qualities whereas Rogier's hard and relentless religiosity forbids any intimate approach.

The contrast is not everywhere equally sharp. Rogier's principal work, II, 53–55 the *Descent from the Cross*, now in the Escorial,[1] fortunately fairly well authenticated, is comparatively close to the work of the Flémalle Master. The emphasis on this close connection is one of the best passages in a book that is full of good passages: Friedrich Winkler's *Der Meister von Flémalle und Rogier* (Strassburg, Heitz, 1913). The *Descent from the Cross* is regarded by most people as a fairly early work. I am inclined to place it at the very beginning. Rogier's father was a sculptor[2] and he came from Louvain. The Escorial panel was painted for Louvain, possibly at Louvain.

The *Portrait of a Woman* that came a few years ago to the Kaiser-
68 Friedrich Museum, Berlin, from St. Petersburg has been added to rather than incorporated in Rogier's *oeuvre*, with some hesitation and not without vigorous protests being raised. Of the few voices worth listening to, Winkler's was notable as clearly affirmative, Hulin's, with less assurance, as negative. Hulin was tentatively in favour of an attribution to the Master of Flémalle.

Before the seated *Female Saint*, a fragment in the National Gallery, London, von Tschudi hesitated between the two masters. The head of this saint is close to the Berlin *Portrait of a Woman*.

As we see, the dividing line is not all too clear and the attempt made by Firmenich-Richartz to amalgamate the two masters though it cannot be approved is at least understandable.[3]

*[1] Now in the Prado, Madrid.   *[2] See p. 17, note 1.
*[3] While most scholars have remained opposed to this amalgamation, the arguments put forward in support of it by E. Renders (*La solution du problème van der Weyden—Flémalle—Campin*, 1931) were not unfavourably received by Friedländer himself in *Die Altniederländische Malerei*, XIV, 1937, pp. 81 ff. A new solution of the problem has been attempted by M. S. Frinta (*The Genius of Robert Campin*, The Hague, 1966), who suggests close collaboration between Campin and Rogier, especially in the Prado *Descent from the Cross*.

There was a Rogier art that flourished in contact with the art of the Flémalle Master before there was a Rogier mannerism. Rogier's early works, probably done soon after 1430, display more freshness, mobility and truth-to-nature than the tense and spiritualized compositions that we think of first when we hear his name.

The oft-copied *Descent from the Cross*, which made the deepest impression II, 53 on his contemporaries and in which the requirements of the Church are better satisfied than in any other Netherlandish altarpiece, seems to reproduce not life but an image. Where Rogier seeks to imitate living things, with insufficient truth-to-nature he does not get beyond the painted image. Here, where the image is his aim, with excessive truth-to-nature he achieves the uncanny effect of living and animated sculpture.

In a shrine that seems just deep enough to accommodate the life-size figures side by side, as long as their movements proceed parallel to the surface of the casing, are eight figures of equal bulk. The idea is that of a relief modeller, frustrating and almost unbearable for the painter. And yet under such compulsion, so restricted, Rogier produced his masterpiece.

The Passion is brought very close to the faithful, thrust before them so remorselessly that they have no possibility of evasion or escape. No distraction, no softening of the impact, no glimpse of any path that leads away from Golgotha. Isolated, remote, the drama of the Passion in the figure group transcends time and space, is eternalized and true to the doctrine of the Church.

In regarding the Escorial panel and the Berlin *Portrait of a Woman* as early works by Rogier I find myself in agreement with Winkler. But I disagree with him about certain other panels and consider myself justified in adding them here. The group, the entity of which is not disputed, is made up as follows—

Vienna, Kunsthistorisches Museum:
    The Madonna standing.   48
    St. Catherine.
        The panels, each only $7\frac{1}{2} \times 4\frac{3}{4}$ in., form a diptych.

London, Collection of Lord Northbrook:[1]
    The Virgin Enthroned, $5\frac{3}{4} \times 4$ in.

Turin, Galleria Sabauda:
    The Visitation.   46
    The Donor's Wing, each $35 \times 14\frac{1}{8}$ in.

*[1] Now in the Schloss Rohoncz Collection (Baron Thyssen), Lugano-Castagnola.

Of the wings, which belonged to the same altarpiece, the *Visitation* is perfectly preserved, the donor has been painted over but the landscape is untouched and most informative.

Luetzschena near Leipzig, Collection of Baron Speck v. Sternburg:[1]
47   *The Visitation*, $22\frac{1}{2} \times 14\frac{1}{4}$ in.

Louvre:
     The Annunciation, $33\frac{7}{8} \times 36\frac{1}{4}$ in.

Antwerp, Royal Museum (Ertborn Collection):
     The Annunciation, $7\frac{7}{8} \times 4\frac{3}{4}$ in.

With reference to the two *Visitations* at Turin and Luetzschena, Winkler expresses the—to me—untenable opinion that they are copies of a lost original by Rogier. If he were right the pictures would have to agree in composition but they could differ in the formal idiom and manner of painting. But the exact opposite is the case. The compositions differ from one another, differ as widely as the identity of the task could possibly permit, style and quality, however, agree throughout: two works, done at approximately the same time by one master, certainly by the same master who executed the small panels in Vienna and London. The two *Annunciations* are slightly weaker.

To begin with I should regard this artist rather as a pupil of the Flémalle Master than of Rogier. The *Annunciation* in the Louvre is reminiscent of the Werle wings by the Master of Flémalle in its spatial construction, in the play of light, in the cast shadow of the sconce. The
48 *Madonna* in Vienna shows surprising similarities to Jan van Eyck, in the movement of the Child and in the fall of the Madonna's mantle. Here the Rogier style does not appear as something adopted or learnt, further developed or modified, rather is it in bud or about to grow rigid.

Our next duty is to compare the group of pictures with the *Descent*
II, 53 *from the Cross* in the Escorial. Winkler seems to have regarded the comparison as hopeless from the start. The delicacy of the former appeared to him so far removed from the 'monumentality' of the celebrated work by Rogier that he despaired of the possibility of bridging the gap. Here, as so often in critical considerations of style, too little account has been taken of the extent to which style is conditioned by size and subject-matter. Admittedly, the violent impact of the *Descent from the Cross* is in sharp contrast to the friendly effect of the *Visitations* and *Madonnas*. But if we compare individual details the results are astonishing. The clear-cut

[1] Now in the Museum of Fine Arts in Leipzig.

head of St. Elizabeth in the *Visitations* at Turin and Luetzschena accords
with the head of the weeping old woman on the extreme left of the
Escorial panel. The drapery of Elizabeth's skirt, particularly in the Turin
picture, corresponds to the drapery of the mourning woman on the
extreme right in the *Descent from the Cross*. The quality—at times badly
underestimated—of the *Visitations* is not inferior to that of the universally
acclaimed Escorial picture. The hand so rich in detail of the Luetzschena
St. Elizabeth is strikingly similar to the famous hand of St. John in the
Escorial. The head of the small Vienna *Madonna* is shaped and rounded
like the women's heads in the *Descent from the Cross*.

There is nothing in the Escorial picture to compare with the landscapes—particularly rich is the background of the sadly neglected donor's
wing at Turin. We must turn to other works by Rogier which I consider
to be somewhat later in date, such as the Vienna triptych with the
Crucifixion. There we find the same rocky, ascending ground, with over- 52
lapping mounds that offer no convenient foothold for the figures, and also
similar cloud formations. In their feeling for landscape the *Visitations*
stand higher than the Vienna altarpiece and higher than any other work
by Rogier. The conception that the further he moved away from the
Master of Flémalle the more meagre and arid his landscape became
explains the superiority of the *Visitations* in my classification, whereas the
assumption that these pictures are the work of a follower of Rogier—still
less of a copyist—breaks down.

The moving *Descent from the Cross*, the soft and blooming *Portrait of a
Woman* in Berlin and the outlined group of pictures give a richly varied
idea of what the master was capable soon after 1432.

Several acknowledged works by Rogier may be dated with some
certainty to around 1450. At that time the artist was in Italy, in Rome
and Ferrara. It is certain that the portrait of Lionello d'Este, belonging
to Mr. M. Friedsam, New York,[1] dates from this time. Probably the altar
panels at Frankfurt and Florence are also of the same period.

The panel at Frankfurt seems Italian in its compositional motif. 57
There is at any rate no other *sacra conversazione* of this kind in the Netherlands. Of the three escutcheons at the bottom two are empty, the third
shows the Florentine fleur-de-lys. In view of the fact that on the right
stand Cosmas and Damian, the saints of the Medici family, and on the
left Peter and John the Baptist, who can be interpreted as the eponymous
saints of Pietro and Giovanni de' Medici, and finally since the panel is

---

*[1] Now in the Metropolitan Museum, New York. The sitter has been identified as Francesco
d'Este, an illegitimate son of Lionello d'Este, by E. Kantorowicz (in *The Journal of the Warburg
and Courtauld Institutes*, III, 1940, pp. 165 ff.).

said to have come to Frankfort from Pisa, it is surely permissible to connect the commission with the Italian journey and date it accordingly.

A similar argument can be applied to the picture of the *Entombment of*
56 *Christ* that has remained in Italy. This again is a composition apparently not connected with Netherlandish tradition. Facius describes the central panel of an altarpiece executed by Rogier at Ferrara in words that fit the picture in Florence: *in media tabula Christus e cruce demissus, Maria mater, Maria Magdalena, Josephus ita expresso dolore, ac lacrimis, ut a vero discrepare non estimes.*

Rogier's art in its 1450 phase can be characterized from the Florentine picture at Frankfort and from the Ferrarese picture in Florence. His personal manner has emerged completely, his style is fully developed, even slightly inflexible. The very fact that he endeavours to assimilate the art of the Southern altarpiece whilst the types and the formal idiom to which he was accustomed remain untouched by the breath of foreign air reveals the firm self-assurance of his character. The figures are sharp and pointed rather than large and monumental. We are unwilling to touch them because everywhere corners protrude and because we are scared of pushing them over. They stand insecurely on the ground. Their limbs diverge. In spite of intensive modelling in the details they have little physical substance and weight as a whole. They seem desiccated and bloodless, with thin limbs narrowing to a point, with joyless careworn heads. In the drapery are many small motifs but little feeling for the material itself. In the colour scheme a primitive local colouring prevails with no apparent interest in the unity of light or mutual accord. The linear element is unusually conspicuous. Contour and inner lines are incisively drawn. Looking back we realize that the further Rogier retreated from the Jan van Eyck and Master of Flémalle orbit the more his types became remote from nature and the more he evolved what we might call a graphic method.

For all that the altar panels executed around 1450 are dominated by an ascetic gravity and an uncompromising stylistic purity which, from an otherwise sensuously oriental art, singles out such distinctive productions as devout in a higher sense and assures them spiritual and intellectual superiority.

I know no other work in which Rogier expresses himself with such impressive eloquence as in the triptych acquired by the Louvre from Lady Theodora Guest. Side by side in archaic, rigid symmetry are the half-length figures of five holy persons: exactly in the centre, in full front view, the threatening sombre form of Christ with wide-open eyes, to the right and to the left in three-quarter profile turning to the centre, first John the Evangelist and the Virgin, and on the wings Mary Magdalen and John 51 the Baptist. Purified and detached from earthly trivialities, here where the task is conceived hieratically, the abstract stylization appears inevitable, the only solution, in no sense a defect or a limitation. The clear, richly detailed landscape is merely a filling for the background. The figures pushed close together conceal the middle ground. No one would dream of asking where exactly in heaven or on earth these figures could dwell.

Rogier's imagination is wholly absorbed by the images of sacred personalities and therefore creative beyond any of his contemporaries in inventing types; he visualizes his creations as a sculptor sees them completely isolated from their environment. The landscape, even though it is constructed with understanding and accurately developed, is an adjunct. Therefore the point where landscape or building on the one hand and the figures on the other meet is a critical one. We would be hard put to find in the master's work a single figure who stands, sits or kneels comfortably or naturally.

As Rogier worked with uniform care throughout and made use of his stock of types untroubled by impressions of nature, it is not too difficult to recognize the works of his mature and late periods. It reflects little credit on art criticism that until quite recently so many of his works could give rise to so much disagreement. It is to be hoped that Winkler's sound and positive book has put an end once and for all to many uncertainties.

The Beaune altarpiece to be sure has never been challenged—perhaps 62–64 only because so few critics have seen it—the triptych with the *Sacraments* 60–61 in the Antwerp museum, painted for Jean Chevrot, incomparably rich in invention and apart from a few male heads perfectly preserved, has been quite unreasonably doubted. A little weaker but nevertheless an original, probably rather later in date, is the *Entombment* in The Hague, which even Winkler criticizes with unjust sharpness.

A work that has seriously prejudiced our idea of Rogier's art must be withdrawn from his *oeuvre*, namely the altarpiece in the Prado known, though with insufficient justification, as the 'Cambrai altarpiece'. This name crops up in all the Rogier literature and in view of the fact that documents referring to an altarpiece commissioned from Rogier in 1452 for Cambrai are known the Madrid work has always received prior, and serious, consideration. Even if—and this is by no means certain —the altarpiece supplied by Rogier to Cambrai should turn out to be the one in Madrid it would not be of much advantage for our understanding of Rogier's art. To all appearances the Madrid panels which constitute the so-called Cambrai altarpiece were executed by a follower of the master, at best then, provided the documents have been correctly interpreted, in Rogier's workshop.[1]

Since Rogier's creative form was not constantly nourished and renewed by direct observation, formulism and routine became an ever-growing threat. The danger was that the master might become his own imitator.

Dated works of the late period authenticated by inscriptions, which could confirm or refute the perhaps rather prejudiced opinions, do not exist. If we feel that a work such as the *Columba* altarpiece in the 58 Pinakothek in Munich, with the crowded *Adoration of the Kings* on the central panel, is a particularly late achievement we are guided by our belief in the above conjectured law.

The relationship of Memlinc to Rogier offers a welcome though not very extensive aid to the dating.

Memlinc takes over compositions and types from Rogier, modestly and 59 in good faith. He knew the Beaune altarpiece, as well as the *Bladelin* and *Columba* altarpieces, or at any rate knew the compositions, from sketches, drawings or copies of them. His style proceeds more from the *Columba* altarpiece than from any other known work of his master. We are inclined to believe that at the very moment when this altarpiece was being produced he was a pupil in Rogier's workshop and helped in its production. It is impossible to determine with any certainty just how long Memlinc remained under the spell of the Brussels master. The nearest one can say is some time between 1455 and 1464, the year of Rogier's death.

The head of the Madonna, the centre of the *Columba* triptych, may be regarded as the prototype of many of Memlinc's Madonnas. Among Rogier's works the large and rather empty *Annunciation*, acquired by Pierpont Morgan from the R. Kann Collection and previously in the Ashburnham Collection,[2] is related to the altarpiece at Munich.

Rogier's active, constructive and systematic mentality condensed the achievements and observations of the Master of Flémalle into formulae. His incisive characterization enabled the pictorial ideas to be transmitted and disseminated abroad by various means and also with the aid of prints. He, more than any other Netherlander of the fifteenth century,

---

*[1] Vrancke van der Stockt, the successor of Rogier as official painter to the city of Brussels, has been identified by Hulin de Loo (in *Biographie nationale de Belgique*, XXIV, 1926–29, col. 66) as the author of the so-called Cambrai altarpiece. This identification has been fully accepted by Friedländer (*Die Altniederländische Malerei*, XIV, 1937, pp. 86 ff.).

*[2] Now in the Metropolitan Museum, New York.

is the true progenitor. Many things derive from him, not only in the Netherlands, but also in France, in Spain and in Germany. His sermon, searching and inspiring even in faulty translations, reverberated far and wide.

A biassed, unjust but pertinent judgment was formulated by Fr. Knapp in an article on the Würzburg art collections.[1] He reproachfully calls the Brussels master the 'Man of Destiny' and holds him responsible for the reversion in Southern Germany to the 'over-stylized Gothic'. A reproach of this nature does more to honour Rogier's inflexible stylistic ideal than do all the tributes otherwise paid to his art.

[1] In the Munich *Jahrbuch*, 1914.

DIERIC BOUTS

VAN MANDER counts Dieric Bouts to the Dutch painters and mentions him together with Ouwater and Geertgen. He found a trace of him at Haarlem. There, in the Cruysstraet, not far from the orphanage, he was shown the house where Dieric Bouts was supposed to have lived. The only painting by the artist that he was able to see—at the house of Gerritsz Buytewegh at Leyden—bore an inscription saying that it had been painted at Louvain in 1462 by Dieric Bouts, a native of Haarlem. As a matter of fact we do find a Dieric Bouts at Louvain who worked for that city between 1450 (?) and 1475 and was twice married.

The documented and accredited work that he executed between 1464 and 1468 for the church of St. Peter at Louvain, the altarpiece of the 81 *Sacrament*, has survived and forms the basis for constructive stylistic criticism.

In view of the master's origin various qualities of his art have from time to time been singled out as national Dutch. The danger of getting caught in a vicious circle is obvious enough when we consider that, apart from Dieric Bouts, we know next to nothing about Dutch painting prior to 1450.

Dieric's style, as we know it in Louvain, is in some respects dependent on Rogier's model. Whether or not we go so far as to assume that Bouts came to Louvain from Haarlem via Brussels, spending some time in Rogier's workshop on the way, the Rogier formula is in any case an element that must be eliminated if we wish to appreciate the personal and the Dutch elements in his style.

The Louvre owns a *Lamentation* which from stylistic evidence can be 77 attributed to Bouts but which in its compositional motifs derives from Rogier. The stiff, rigid body of Christ lying diagonally on the Virgin's lap is—unnaturally—turned to the front, towards the picture surface, in a manner similar to that in Rogier's altarpiece of the *Virgin* at Granada.

In the altarpiece at Granada and in the altarpiece of *St. John* in Berlin, the Brussels master developed a particular type of altarpiece. The main scenes are enclosed in a Gothic portal framework and the painted sculpture, in the small groups of the intrados, contains a rich narrative material. I do not doubt that this mode of composition was very much in the spirit of Rogier and even if he did not actually invent it he certainly developed and popularized it (around 1440). Bouts adopted this type of composition in his triptych at Valencia (replica at Granada)[1] and in four altar panels of the same size in the Prado. The figure of the Rising Christ 72–75 at Valencia is modelled on the small figure in the background in Rogier's altarpiece of the *Virgin*.

The connection with the Brussels master makes it probable that we have here relatively early works of the Louvain master, particularly as his chief work, executed in the 60's, is not so clearly reminiscent of the prototype.

A study of the four panels in the Prado enables us to define the relationship even more precisely. We note a connection with Rogier in superficialities, the following of a fashion. Perhaps the commission required portals and portal sculpture. The style, unaffected by Rogier, seems to be Dieric's personal style in an otherwise unknown, certainly early, Dutch phase.

I imagine that about 1440 Bouts, as a mature artist, left Haarlem for the West, that he was not trained in Rogier's studio but that he did succumb to the art dominating Brussels and radiating to Louvain at that time, gradually, however, freeing himself from the pressure.

The pictures in the Prado represent *The Annunciation*, *The Visitation*, *The* 72–75 *Nativity* and *The Adoration of the Kings*. Certain parts have been crudely retouched. The *Annunciation* is well preserved, except for the white robe of the Angel. In the *Visitation* wide areas have been worked over such as the red robe of St. Elizabeth and part of the blue one of the Virgin, part of the landscape, almost the entire ground. Notably the head of the Virgin is well preserved. In the *Nativity* the head of the Child has been touched up; ground, landscape, sky, heads are intact. The *Adoration of the Kings* is the best preserved.

The figures are short with massive heads, far removed from the leanness and the jagged, widespread contours of the Rogier forms, differing too from the rigidly taut figures that Bouts favoured in the 60's. The folds are simple, not nearly so conspicuous as Rogier's drapery lines. The observation penetrates lovingly to the details and in certain bits, such as the hands of the oldest king in the *Adoration*, comes startlingly close to nature. The texture—brocades, hair—is rendered with almost Eyckian passion. The panels as a whole are far more humane and warm-blooded than anything of Rogier's, more too than Bouts elsewhere. Though some

*[1] According to Friedländer's later view (as expressed in *Die Altniederländische Malerei*, XIV, 1937, p. 90) the Granada version is the original and the Valencia triptych a smaller, but very exact replica produced in the master's workshop.

general and familiar characteristics of the Bouts idiom emerge clearly enough in his female types, such as the short noses, the small, apparently blinking eyes, the strong reflecting lights, particularly striking in the head of the Virgin Annunciate, yet the confidence, intimacy and archaism dispel any idea of imitation. Everything accords with the theory that Bouts developed this style in Holland. The impression of space is convincing as is the uniform treatment of light with cast shadows and colour perspective. At this stage Bouts is scarcely affected by the fatal emphasis on line. The landscape—it is convenient to compare the *Visitation* with 73,46,47 the similarly composed *Visitations* by Rogier at Turin and Luetzschena— is homely, inviting and exists in its own right. The happy atmosphere is as much opposed to the resigned mood that Bouts subsequently revealed as it is to the bitter pathos of Rogier.

Ouwater has been wrongly suggested as the author of the Madrid panels but the mistake is instructive. The only known work by Ouwater is not, in fact, so very different though admittedly far weaker and less 86 substantial.[1] If Ouwater, who worked at Haarlem, did stand in any relationship to Bouts then the contact must have been with the early Haarlem style of his compatriot and our idea of the Prado panels is confirmed. I believe, incidentally, that Ouwater was stimulated by Bouts and that one would not be justified in reversing the relationship.

It was quite wrong to uphold the attribution to Petrus Christus of the Prado panels wherein at least their archaism and closeness to Van Eyck were rightly perceived.

The centre panel of the Altarpiece of the *Sacrament* completed in 1468, 81 which has remained at Louvain and which is slightly higher than broad, represents the *Last Supper*. The clear disposition of the interior allows plenty of room for the gathering; it has natural height, is constructed correctly in perspective and makes quite a convincing impression apart from the fact that the vanishing point is rather high. In front, a fairly broad strip of the richly patterned tiled floor remains empty which increases the illusion of depth in the interior. The spacious hall is illuminated in a uniform and consistent way from two windows on the left.

Christ is exactly in the centre and seen from the front. The Apostles, who are distinguished from one another mainly by the shape of their beards and their hair styles, are seated symmetrically on the right and on the left but with some agreeable deviations in the symmetry. The

85 [1] Another painting considered by Friedländer (in *Die Altniederländische Malerei*, III, 1925, pp. 61 and 112) as a fragment of a work by Ouwater is the *Head of a Donor* in the Metropolitan Museum, New York.

Saviour as a type is not unlike Rogier's heads of Christ but with less intellectual power, less compelling, more a sufferer, used to suffering, with less strongly accentuated nostrils and a look which—instead of Rogier's threatening stare—seems to implore. The whole mood is subdued and elegiac, in no way dramatically tense, something in the nature of a conventicle of pious and well-behaved men, a memorial celebration that will be repeated from time to time.

The wings—those in Berlin well preserved, those in Munich ruined in parts by restoration[1]—provide a strong contrast to the central panel. The story tells how while Elijah sleeps an angel comes with food and bends over him, how Abraham and Melchisedek meet, how the Jews take the Passover meal standing, ready for the journey, and how they gather manna in the wilderness. The narrative is neither concise nor searching. The painter's aim to depict strange and remote events gives a particular charm to the scenes, even though each detail is fashioned after nature with patient objectivity and sincere humility. The tense and rather heavy atmosphere results less from certain peculiarities in the costumes than from the deep colouring and from the landscape. Bouts boldly attempted evening light and colourful sunsets. Transparent distances, shadowy masses of foliage, hills shutting out the light—all play their part.

The intermediate position of the Louvain master between Jan van Eyck and Rogier—and this is in no way meant to suggest a chronological order or a school relationship—becomes really clear the moment we compare the portraits. Bouts frequently and willingly introduced portraits into his compositions just as he loved to follow the model conscientiously and faithfully. The altarpiece of *The Last Supper* includes a series of portrait heads, though to the detriment of the picture as a whole insofar as the other heads appear over-stereotyped in comparison.[2] The *Judgment* panels 78–79 in the Brussels museum contain a whole gallery of portraits. Evidently the Governors of Louvain had themselves perpetuated here. There is no lack of donor portraits in the master's devotional pictures. Perhaps the finest is in the panel with Christ and John the Baptist, belonging to Prince Leuchtenberg at Schloss Seeon (Bavaria).[3] Single portraits are very rare. Apart from the generally accepted *Portrait of a Man* dated 1462 in the 83, 84 National Gallery, London, the *Portrait of a Man* in the Metropolitan

---

*[1] The wings are now again joined to the centre panel in the Church of S. Pierre at Louvain.

*[2] The altarpiece was commissioned by the Confraternity of the Holy Sacrament of St. Peter's Church on March 15, 1464, and, according to Professor J. G. van Gelder (in *Oud-Holland*, LXVI, 1951, p. 51), the portraits are those of the four masters of the Confraternity whose names appear in the contract of 1464.

*[3] Later in the collection of Prince Rupprecht of Bavaria (died 1955).

Museum, New York (formerly belonging to Baron A. Oppenheim and Mr. B. Altman) is especially characteristic in the cut of the head, the steepness of which is further accentuated by a high cap. To these I may add a small portrait belonging to Mr. E. Warneck, Paris[1] (Exposition Toison d'or in Bruges, Plate 37 of the exhibition publication) and— though with less confidence—the *Bust of an Elderly Man* exhibited by Mr. A. Brown at the Guildhall, London, in 1906 (No. 4, as by Van Eyck, reproduced in the exhibition catalogue).[2] How freely set in space and lightly detached from the background is the portrait of 1462! There is comparatively much that is individual in this portrait, also in the others, although the kind and rather depressed humanity, inherent in all the master's human beings, radiates through. The heads are angular, and long straight lines, contours and furrows give something careworn to the expression. The line is emphasized, less in the early works, most strongly in the very late *Judgment* panels, but it has a different function from that in Rogier's art. Dieric's lines are ploughed shadows and reflecting strips but never merely graphic lines of demarcation such as Rogier, particularly in his late period, used so ruthlessly. Bouts would never, for instance, draw the far side of the face, that should recede into the depth, sharply silhouetted against the background.

Apart from the *Sacrament* altarpiece, so rich in content, only one other

78-79 work by Dieric is authenticated with any certainty, namely the two companion pieces now in the Brussels museum, which relate rather vaguely a forgotten error of justice and, in accordance with the custom of the time, were hung in the town hall of Louvain as a warning to the judges. We learn that towards the end of his life Bouts worked for the city and that after his death in 1475 Hugo van der Goes, of Ghent, was called to Louvain to give an expert opinion on how far the pictures had progressed and what should be paid for the finished parts. Therefore Dieric's death had interrupted the work. The condition of the pictures agrees with the documentary evidence once we examine the Brussels panels carefully.

The *Judgment* pictures have been sharply criticized and the blame laid (not without some justification) on the size that is too big, and on the subject that was not congenial to him, but the parts for which Bouts was not responsible have never been separated from the rest.

The first panel represents the unjust execution of the Count who has

---

*[1] Now in the Metropolitan Museum, New York. X-ray examination, which has revealed a hand (of a patron saint?) resting on the sitter's shoulder, has established the fact that this portrait is a fragment from a larger panel.

*[2] Now in the National Gallery of Art, Washington (Samuel H. Kress Collection).

been falsely accused by the Empress. The second panel shows the Countess with the red-hot iron in her hand testifying to the innocence of the executed man, with the Empress consumed by flames in the background. The second panel appears to have been completely finished by Bouts but the lower half of the first was apparently unfinished when Bouts died and was clumsily and crudely filled in. The ridiculous figure of the man standing at the edge of the picture on the extreme left and the drapery of the kneeling Countess are certainly not by Dieric.

Whereas the large panels seem empty and expose the painful nerveless-ness of the long figures as well as the weakness in their grouping, an unusually small size is advantageous for this art.

In the Munich Pinakothek a small altarpiece with the *Adoration of the Kings* in the centre, *St. John the Baptist* and *St. Christopher* on the wings, has 80 long been attributed to Dieric; for this work one is trying to retain the old-fashioned name 'Pearl of Brabant'. In recent art literature we find frequent attempts to remove the 'Pearl' from the Louvain masters' 'jewels'. Other small-size devotional pictures in the style of Bouts have been associated with the Munich triptych and a special master, a follower of Bouts, constructed. As far as I can see, this attempt to create an inde-pendent personality capable of existing next to Bouts has not been success-ful. The small size in itself conveys an impression of daintiness. The composition seems lighter and more pleasing, the figures move with greater freedom. The intensive and fiery local colours press closer together over smaller areas, which produces a vivid interplay of colour. For the rest, form, colour, conception, types and everything else are in complete accord with the accepted Bouts style which can best be verified in Munich itself where the triptych and the *Sacrament* altarpiece hang side by side.[1] I do not even believe that there is any considerable time interval between the *Sacrament* altarpiece and the 'Pearl of Brabant'.

Dieric's talent was not sufficiently robust and comprehensive to create out of his own resources an outstandingly impressive group, to make a movement flow through every limb of a body; but his devout and careful method of working could successfully fashion and animate a head or a hand. We sense the love of plant life and landscape as an essential and personal trait. Delight in his true perception of the colour and nature of the individual detail is blended with emotion at the touchingly awkward and halting co-ordination of the whole.

*[1] The wings of the *Sacrament* altarpiece are now again at Louvain, see p. 29 note 1.

HUGO VAN DER GOES

THE size of a picture and the scale of the figures have their share in determining method and style of the painter. Compelled by some commission probably every Netherlandish painter of the fifteenth century undertook small, medium and large-sized panels and, to a greater or lesser degree according to his nature, yielded to the dictates of the size on his style. In many cases art critics were unable to surmount the obstacle of a change of scale and, confused by the difference in style resulting from this change, failed to perceive the identity of the artists, as in the case of Dieric Bouts. A particular size is suitable and natural for every talent even though adaptability to a greater or lesser degree must be assumed and is apparent. Generally speaking a small size is appropriate for early Netherlandish panel painting, which is akin to miniature painting. And for the production of not a few Netherlandish painters the verdict stands: the quality rises and falls in 'inverse proportion' to the measurements of the picture. This certainly applies to Petrus Christus and to the Bruges painter whom we call Adriaen Ysenbrandt. Others, among them famous masters, do not pass unscathed beyond a medium size, as for instance Memlinc and Gerard David, whose religious works done for Spanish patrons (the organ panels from Najera in the Antwerp Museum and the altarpiece of *St. Anne* in the J. E. Widener Collection, Philadelphia[1]) are felt to be too big. Here as in many other cases the feeling intrudes that we are looking at enlarged rather than large figures, the uneasy feeling that execution and size are not suited to one another, that the knowledge of form, the observation and content do not suffice to fill out the enlarged boundaries.

Dieric Bouts seems to grow timid as soon as he approaches life-size. His, as it were, short-sighted piecemeal method of execution shies at extensive surfaces. As regards inventive power and conception, Memlinc and Gerard David seem more able to cope with large surfaces but not as regards the formal content. Finally there is a mysterious connection between intellectual power and picture size. Only if his talent is profound and deep-rooted has the artist the power to fill large surfaces of a canvas

---

*[1] Now in the National Gallery of Art, Washington.

in such a way that the proportions appear natural and that no disturbing contrast arises between content and form.

Hugo van der Goes gave wings to Eyckian painting and made it supple enough to cover wide spaces. Conception and execution, all creative forces are ample, they combine and radiate from the centre of his personality to produce a monumentality that is new in Netherlandish panel painting and of a different order from what we might describe as monumentality in certain productions by the Master of Flémalle and by Rogier.

A clear conception of the art of Hugo van der Goes was late in coming, a fine success for constructive stylistic criticism. For a long time the Portinari altarpiece in Florence, authenticated from Vasari's account as a work by the Ghent master, stood isolated amidst the Florentine altar panels, a strangely moving work in its harsh sincerity. Many art lovers returning to the North from Florence with the expected impressions, and this unexpected one, sought in vain for other works by the great Netherlandish artist. Scheibler was the first to make serious efforts to trace the style of the Portinari altarpiece. His was the hardest task. In his doctor thesis of 1880 he made the following claim, paradoxical at the time but valid today: "Hugo van der Goes is equal in quality to every one of Van Eyck's successors and as prolific as the majority of them."

The altarpiece which he made for Tommaso Portinari can be dated by 88–93 the number and ages of the children portrayed on the wings approximately to the years 1475–76. This large work must have been begun considerably earlier. Perhaps Goes, who is documented at Bruges in 1468, already at that time came in contact with Tommaso Portinari, who was living there as the agent of the Medici. He became free master at Ghent in 1467 and died in 1482. The Portinari altarpiece is a work of his middle period and therefore suitable as a crystallization point. The vast dimensions, to satisfy the Florentine demands, exceed what was usual in the North, but for the Ghent master they served as a stimulus, as an opportunity to give his powers full scope rather than as a compulsion or restraint. The central panel is some 10 ft. wide by 8 ft. 2 in. high. And not only are the panel boards long and wide, not only do the human beings attain life-size but the figures in themselves achieve a corresponding weight and cubic bulk and the three-dimensional space recedes in accordance with the surface extension of the picture plane. Atmospheric depth is captured by a compositional method of revolutionary audacity. The relief form has been dropped. The relationships between the figures and the groups do not develop along the picture plane, or parallel to it, but pressing forward out of the depth and driving into the depth they intersect in the Christ child, whose feeble frame is the centre and goal of the adoration pouring in from all sides. The middle ground is no longer empty and dead. The gradual reduction in scale of the figures is supported by the gradation of the colour values. The solemnity, the significance of the event, the inner dignity and spiritual nobility of the figures seem to constitute the deeper content of the whole.

In general, the figures in fifteenth-century Netherlandish devotional panels are felt to be members of one family or society, and the donors, introduced by their patron saints, are admitted as equals into the holy circle. In the Portinari altarpiece a dualism is intensified to dramatic effect. The people, the 'third estate', represented in the shepherds, press forward to salvation and their rough lowliness, inspired with zealous faith, blends with the dignity of the saints and the lean spirituality of the angels so that the ultimate and supreme conception unites a richly contrasted community. With the shepherds a new kind of piety, drawn from the congregation, is elevated to the altarpiece, a coarse and lumbering rapture that is ennobled by emotion and touching devotion.

In the large dimensions Goes, as a skilled craftsman, achieves a convincing illusion of solidity whilst as a painter, guided by his observation of light and colour values, he lets the form take shape.

The illusion of solidity, it is true, is everywhere evoked by contrasts of light. But we can construct a difference and distinguish between two methods of production—to take one extreme we might put it thus: from his imagination and experience a painter can successfully direct the light and allow it to flow in such a way that the form emerges, he can take just as much from his observation of light as he requires to represent form, that is to say with measured care and preconceived judgment he can exploit his power of observation for his work. At the other extreme we have the painter who has, or wishes to have, no preconceived idea of the form, but abandons himself completely to observation and lets the illusion take shape in colours, dabs of colour and light values. Naturally these extremes do not exist as such but it is possible to set up a scale between them and to allot a particular place to each painter. Let no one maintain that only the methods differ but that the results are the same. Light fulfils the task of making form visible in the same way that rain fulfils the task of watering the fields, it does not function for this purpose and only at times produces this result. Just as rain sometimes floods the fields, so light sometimes destroys, confuses or distorts the illusion of form capriciously, irrationally. Our established contrast is also of importance for the results.

If on the one hand pure and absolute observation leads to confused forms every limitation of observation on the other hand brings impoverishment and schematization.

On the whole, painting has tended to develop ever closer to the second extreme as its ideal, that is to say there has been an increasing tendency, come what may, to stick to the capricious illusion so that every more recent picture would give an impression of anarchy to a fifteenth-century eye whereas every picture of the fifteenth century seems schematic to the modern eye.

Van der Goes made a tremendous advance in the direction of the second extreme and, after the Van Eycks, he is the greatest pioneer in Netherlandish panel painting of the fifteenth century.

The master envelops wide areas in chiaroscuro. The light in his pictures picks out some forms, represses others, emphasizes, dissolves, loosens, divides and unites. He searches out reflexes that are hostile to form and draws more of the infinite wealth of nature into his picture than is observed by any other painter of his period.

Goes seems to have studied nature out of doors. His colour is strikingly cool. He avoids brownish shadows in the flesh tones. Grey, transparent tones generally produce the fleeting transient play of light on the flesh that gives the effect of material and is astonishingly varied in the local colouring of the complexion.

Nothing could better designate the avantgarde position of the master than the mistake made by one of our leading art critics who, when the *Nativity* came to Berlin, expressed the opinion that it was clearly a work 98 of the sixteenth century, and therefore could not be by Van der Goes.

The road that the master traversed before he reached the Portinari altarpiece (and he went still further) is not entirely hidden from us. Scheibler attributed to him the three small panels in Vienna. *Adam and Eve, The Lamentation over Christ* and *St. Genevieve*, which form a diptych. 94–95 This attribution can be accepted with the proviso that the date of origin must lie considerably before 1475. In the first place, however, the effect of the dimensions must be taken into account. The incisive and variegated colour effect of these panels is partly conditioned by their size. Penetrating to the depth, searching out bones and sinews, the draughtsman works with a conscientiousness that borders on self-torment. The contour lines are exceedingly nervous. Restricted by the size, Goes does not evolve the self-assured freedom of the Portinari altarpiece. But in my opinion the strenuous ascetic intensity of the Vienna pictures is in some measure due to the awkwardness and zeal of youth. If we compare them with the

triptych of the *Adoration of the Kings* in the collection of Prince Liechtenstein, Vienna,[1] which is no bigger, a considerable divergency in style
is apparent. Here, too, we sense the pressure of the restricted size but
the pressure works in a different direction. In the triptych the master
seems to be confronted with an unexpected obstacle, constrained by the
smallness of the panels he cannot organize the available space, but the
drawing is nothing like so incisive, detailed and finical in style as it is in
the diptych where the painter adapted composition and execution to suit
the size. I do not regard the triptych in the Liechtenstein gallery at all as
an early work.

Very close to the Vienna diptych is the small *Madonna* in Frankfurt
87 (the wings are obviously not by Van der Goes). I consider this picture to
be one of the earliest known works of the master.

Apart from the Portinari altarpiece we know two other works by Goes
the dates of which can be fairly accurately established without the aid of
stylistic criticism. In all probability the Ghent master was commissioned
to do the donor wing of the Bouts altarpiece at Bruges immediately after
Dieric's death, that is directly after 1476. The altar wings at Holyrood
with the portraits of James III of Scotland and his son were made about
1478 or at any rate not very much later. The prince, the future James
IV, who is depicted as a boy, was born in 1473. Incidentally I do not
believe that Goes completed the portraits of Scottish Royalty but that
they were inserted by a weak hand, probably a painter in Scotland. I
assume that Sir Edward Bonkil, whose portrait as donor is obviously by
100 Van der Goes, had commissioned the panel in the Netherlands and that
the monarch to whom he dedicated them had his portrait and that of his
wife added.

The wing panels in Scotland are not only related in style to the
Portinari altarpiece, they are also of equal quality. But it is essential to
distinguish what is genuine from what is not. In the panel with the king
the dusky red tent is well preserved, as are the architecture and the
wooden cross of St. Andrew. The head of the apostle is not quite intact,
his green gown, his book and hands have been considerably overpainted.
The king's head need not be considered here, as presumably even in its
original condition it did not derive from Goes. The king's dress and book
are passably well preserved but his hands are spoilt, as is also the ver-
milion gown of the young prince. The Trinity has been energetically
'restored' and only the greater part of the body of Christ, the loincloth

*[1] The collection has been transferred from Vienna to Vaduz in Liechtenstein, but several
paintings, amongst them the *Adoration* by Hugo van der Goes, have for several years been on loan
to the National Gallery, London.

and the Dove still reveal the hand of the master. The wing with the Queen is better where St. George seems fully intact, and, finest of all, relatively well preserved, is the picture with the clerical donor and the organ-playing angels. The quality here is as fine as Goes achieved anywhere and it can be enjoyed unspoilt, especially in the hand and in the magnificent gown of the donor.

The *Nativity* in Berlin differs so much from the Florentine altarpiece 98 that every critic feels that a time interval must separate the two. But strangely enough there seems to be no consensus of opinion as to which is the older. And the view I expressed in 1903 on the relative dates has not been accepted. I wrote, amongst other things, on the Berlin picture:[1]

"The *Nativity* with the Shepherds and the Angels, the same subject as in the central panel of the Portinari altarpiece, is depicted here. This makes the comparison easier. We are thus more quickly able to overcome our amazement and can reach a comparatively reliable, positive and negative verdict more easily. The Berlin panel is almost 8 ft. 2 in. wide and not quite 3 ft. 3 in. high. The dire necessity of spreading the familiar scene over such a wide area stimulated the artist to compositional ingenuities. The Florentine picture with its more convenient and natural proportions gives an incomparably greater effect of space but the grouping of the figures seems meagre, sparse and awkward whereas our picture is relief-like, devoid of air and overloaded but flowing and dynamic though less unified in composition than the Portinari panel. It is as if we were reading the narrative which is unfolded before us in epic sequence and the sections are filled with a variety of moods. Pathos alternates with noble calm. The limited space and the habitual arrangement of a triptych may have first suggested the striking and unique motif, may have given the master the significant idea, which is rooted in ancient typological conceptions, namely that of placing a chorus in front of the pictorial scene. On the right and on the left the representation is powerfully framed by the half-figure of a prophet whose approximately life-sized form looms in almost frightening contrast to the figures in the central scene who are only half as large. The prophets with deeply lined faces, visionary eyes and pointing gestures unveil the picture by drawing back a curtain. Dangerously theatrical devices have been used to endow the oft-repeated scene with a heightened meaning, to isolate it from the ordinary world.

"Two-fifths of the panel width are cleverly filled by the figures of the prophets but in spite of this the picture space seems rather low in comparison to its width. Beneath the low roof the figures kneel, bend and

[1] In the journal *Kunst und Künstler*.

incline towards the Christ Child. The compulsion of the form blends with
the demands of the subject. The shepherds approach from the left in
eager haste. An invisible barrier seems to separate the kneeling figure of
the Virgin mother from this passionate and needy throng of humanity.
Joseph is saying his prayers before the Christ Child with ritual solemnity.
A group of youthful angels, of somewhat uniform beauty, pressed together
head to head, fill the empty spaces.

"The colour is rich, on the whole rather cool and almost variegated, in
certain parts of exquisite harmony, everywhere pregnant with meaning,
like the musical accompaniment to the formal theme. To the right and
to the left near the edges heavy, warm colours predominate, a sumptuous
dusky red in the dress of one of the prophets and a brilliant scarlet in the
cloak of the other; the shepherds are clad in garments of less pure, broken
and iridescent hues, which relegates their importunate need to a subordinate place. Joseph is dressed all in red, a rather sharp blueish dark red
in the outer garment and a dull brownish orange in the under-garment.
The main group in the centre, on the other hand, is entirely steeped in
the cool colours of the sky, white and blue with faint shades of violet.
The whitish rather chalky complexion, lightly shaded with grey, of the
Virgin, the Christ Child and the angels harmonizes with the dull ash
blond hair and heightens the effect of unearthliness and transfiguration.
The slight physical form of the new-born Child is drawn with relentless
realism and yet His divine nature is evoked with dark symbolism in
significant gestures and in the mature, spiritualized countenance. Perhaps
too the intensely thoughtful master, who ever sought to link the individual
and the earthly to the universal and the divine may have introduced the
sheaf of corn as something more than a *repoussoir*. In the drawing and
modelling, especially of the hands, Van der Goes shows an amazing
mastery, almost too much mastery. He is in full possession of his powers
on the downward rather than on the upward grade. Compared with the
robust vigour that seems amazed at its own strength in the Portinari
altarpiece, a weary confidence seems to lie over our picture. For this
reason I am inclined to place our panel and also the *Death of the Virgin* at
Bruges, which is if anything a degree more artificial, confident and
virtuoso, later, after the Portinari altarpiece. Though if Hugo van der
Goes died in 1482—and the Florentine altarpiece can hardly have been
done before 1475—there is admittedly not much margin to spare. These
dates, however, appear firmly fixed. Since in the Berlin altarpiece the
gentle and rather generalized beauty of the Virgin and the angels evoke
the age of Memlinc and Gerard David—by contrast the figures in the

Portinari altarpiece seem lean and ageing—whilst the bold unbroken flux of the composition even suggests Quentin Massys, we are certainly justified in dating the work as late as possible."

I see no reason to modify these observations of 1903. My task is rather to examine and defend the conclusions that I drew from them in the light of the Monforte panel, still unknown to me in 1903, which has appeared as a major work alongside the *Nativity* and which in its turn requires to 99
be inserted chronologically.

Unfortunately I am unable to welcome the new guest triumphantly as the missing link whose existence I had intuitively suspected. New difficulties arise but no clarification. The Monforte panel does not seem to fit into the constructed line of development.

In its spatial effect, in the rich free treatment of light the Monforte *Adoration of the Kings* is closer to the Portinari altarpiece than to the *Nativity*. The intellectual and formal harmony, the full, even opulent colour, the superb confidence of the modelling, the naturalness of the drapery, in which angular, rectilinear folds are done away with, all this makes me hesitate to date the Monforte panel before the Portinari altarpiece, as has been suggested by at least one scholar. The most likely position for the *Adoration* seems to lie between the Florentine panel and the *Nativity*. I must admit though that this order too is far from satisfactory and does not give at all a picture of organic growth.

The panel with the *Death of the Virgin*, owing to foolish judgment of its 101
state, has been fantastically misunderstood. Nowhere does the master express himself more clearly, at least as a draughtsman and in the psychology. The subject seems to determine the style and even more the colour. It is as though Van der Goes was led to make a new approach for each work, depending on the mood of the theme. Thus in the present case, cold and unsensuous as it is in the colour, all the expressive force is concentrated in the drawing of the heads and of the hands. To an even greater degree than in the Portinari altarpiece observation has been replaced by experience, not strongly enough to entitle us to speak of a mannerism but far enough for us to recognize his own particular handwriting in the even waviness of the contours. The Apostles with fully developed character heads have their share in a heightened sensitiveness that borders on monomania. Their piety is not pure and calm but rather the faith of penitents oppressed by memories. A dangerous passion is concealed in their agony, almost as though at the death-bed of the Virgin self-accusation and repentance mingled with their grief.

The *Death of the Virgin* and the Portinari altarpiece reveal the searching, struggling soul of their author. Here more than in any other work of the fifteenth century is a personal avowal. Here the art critic must turn psychologist and eagerly grasp at the report of Hugo's mental disorder as offering some explanation and confirmation.

Goes left Ghent, where he had enjoyed honorary offices in the guild until 1473, and spent the last years of his life in the monastery of Roodende near Brussels. This step is in itself highly suggestive, and in addition intimate details are supplied in a chronicle written by a certain Gaspar Offhuys, who was a novice when the painter entered the monastery.[1] In this account Goes is depicted as a celebrity who enjoyed special privileges in the monastic life and who had by no means completely renounced either his work as a painter or the vanities of the world. Goes received visits from the high nobility, including Archduke Maximilian (the future Emperor Maximilian), was not averse to wine and was often a victim of fits of melancholy that sometimes mounted to delirium, to the manic idea that he was doomed to perdition.

Perhaps Goes placed himself under monastic discipline as a protection against his own passions, perhaps he was driven into the ecclesiastical stronghold by religious scruples. The excesses noted in the philistine report suggest if not a pathological then at least a problematic nature.

Were we to read that Petrus Christus had become mentally unbalanced there would be no reason to draw any conclusions from the circumstance. But in the art of Hugo van der Goes we sense such a tremendous tension that the break, the disorder of his mind, appears as the result of his creative work or else the productions of his genius are the result of an abnormal tendency.

Even an expert pathologist could probably not go much beyond these amateur phrases, particularly as the medical report of the fifteenth century though fairly wordy is crudely interspersed with superstitious prejudices and moralizing warnings.

*[1] He may have entered the monastery in 1478. In March 1478 he was still paying rent for his house at Ghent (A. de Schryver, in *Gentsche Bijdragen*, XVI, 1955/56, p. 193). As he died in 1482, this fact agrees with the statement of Offhuys that Van der Goes spent the last five or six years of his life in the monastery (see F. Winkler, *Das Werk des Hugo van der Goes*, Berlin 1964, p. 1).

III. MEMLINC: *The Annunciation to the Shepherds*. Detail from the 'Seven Joys of Mary'. Munich, Alte Pinakothek

HANS MEMLINC

WE possess many works of Memlinc, more than of any other Netherlander of the fifteenth century. His art is conveniently accessible. Together at Bruges are undisputed works by his hand, some of which are signed. They make a deep impression there, like the fairest home-grown bloom—even though the master was not a native of the town—and their charm was felt even when the general understanding of Netherlandish painting was still in embryo.

The master's *oeuvre* has increased and has continued to increase year by year. Niggling criticism has had little success. The *oeuvre* remained close-knit, composed of similar parts with nowhere a gap into which the critical knife could be inserted.

Memlinc is documented at Bruges as early as 1466[1] where he worked until his death in 1494 apparently without any considerable interruptions. As he is almost always referred to as Hans not Jan we are justified in regarding him as of German origin. The diary of Rombout de Doppere, a notary of the church of St. Donatian, Bruges, contains under the year 1494 the following entry: *Die XI augusti, Brugis obiit magister Johannes Memmelinc, quem praedicabant peritissimum fuisse et excellentissimum pictorem totius tunc orbis christiani. Oriundus erat Mogunciaco* (Mainz), *sepultus Brugis ad aegidii.* Since there is a village Mömlingen in the Mainz area we can assume that the master, or at any rate his family, came from that place.[1]

To establish the year of his birth we have only the unreliable clue to his age contained in a self-portrait presumably painted in 1468. It is at least probable that the altarpiece which he painted for the Englishman 110–111 John Donne, owned by the Duke of Devonshire (now at Chatsworth),[2] originated in 1468, when the wedding of Charles the Bold and Margaret of York was being celebrated at Bruges, for which occasion distinguished Englishmen in close touch with the court came to Bruges, and I consider it certain that the man standing modestly behind the pillar on the left wing of the altarpiece, near his patron saint John the Baptist, is a self-portrait. If we note that Memlinc looks about thirty-five here, we can

---

*[1] From an entry in the Bruges Burgesses' Book published by R. A. Parmentier (*Indices op de Brugsche Poorterboeken*, Bruges 1938, I, p. xxxvi) it is now known that Memlinc was born at Seligenstadt, a small town in the Mainz area, and became a burgess at Bruges on January 30, 1465.

*[2] Now in the National Gallery, London.

infer from this that he was born about 1433 though admittedly the conclusion is rather doubtful. But we have no better means of establishing
the year of his birth.

Our only knowledge of the master's fortunes before he came to Bruges
and began his steady, prolific and well-rewarded activity, is deduced
from his style. Rogier's art is the foundation of Memlinc's art. Rogier
was Memlinc's teacher. This is as certain as any such relationship can be
certain when deduced only from stylistic criticism.[1] Rogier died in
Brussels in 1464, in 1466 Memlinc is first documented at Bruges.[2] Our
next assumption is that Memlinc, before he went to Bruges, worked for
some time at Brussels in the studio of the leading master there. This
assumption is rather weakened when we note that between 1470 and
1490 art at Bruges as a whole was under Rogier's sway, that the Eyckian
tradition which did not obviously influence Memlinc's style was everywhere pushed into the background at Bruges.

There are connecting links between the works of Rogier and Memlinc.
Memlinc adopted several of Rogier's compositions.

The masters are by no means similar in temperament. They were
certainly not kindred spirits. Memlinc's dependence is explained most
easily and naturally by the authority of the master and the community
of the studio.

As far as we can see, Memlinc knew and used Rogier's *Columba* altar-
58 piece, at that time at Cologne (now in Munich), both the central panel
with the *Adoration of the Kings* and the right wing with the *Presentation
of Christ in the Temple;* furthermore he knew the Middelburg Altarpiece
59 (Berlin), from which he borrowed at least the drapery motif of the
62 Madonna, and finally the altarpiece at Beaune. His *Crucifixion* (Vicenza)
was taken from the Brussels master but in this case it is not possible to
establish the particular model, seeing that Rogier often repeated the
subject with slight variations. These connections are easy to explain on
the assumption that Memlinc worked for a time in Rogier's studio,
without this assumption they become difficult. In Rogier's studio the
younger master could easily have copied preparatory drawings for altarpieces which had long since left the studio. As a matter of fact we are not
exclusively limited to observations of style if we wish to define the
relationship more precisely. In an inventory of the art treasures of
Margaret of Austria compiled in 1516 we find the following entry:
Ung petit tableaul d'ung dieu de pityé estant ès bras de Nostre-Dame; ayant

*[1] For Friedländer's later views on this subject see his *Memling* (Amsterdam 1949), where he
gave further proofs of the relationship.
*[2] See p. 41, note 1.

deux feulletz, dans chascun desquelz y a ung ange es dessus lesdits feulletz y a une
annunciade de blanc et de noir. Fait, le tableaul, de la main de Rogier, et lesdits
feulletz, de celle de maistre Hans.

If this entry is to be believed then the triptych was produced in Rogier's
workshop with the collaboration of Memlinc.

No picture like the one described here, the small central panel: *Christ*
as Man of Sorrows in the arms of the Virgin, is known by Rogier but there
is one by Memlinc. Two panels, one at Granada and one privately 108
owned in France (dated 1475),[1] would fit the description. In view of the
Memlinc panels we might conclude that the inventory of 1516 was mistaken, not only the two wings but also the central panel were the work
of Memlinc and identical with the picture privately owned in France.
We can, however, and with more justification believe the inventory,
regard the Rogier panel as lost and reconstruct its appearance from the
Memlinc pictures.

In the small Sforza altarpiece in the Brussels gallery, which has recently
been attributed to Bugati, an Italian painter who was apprenticed to
Rogier, Memlinc characteristics have been rightly discerned within the
strictly Rogierian workshop style. I consider it unlikely that Bugati could
have completely effaced his national style. He cannot even be considered
as the author. On the other hand I think it possible that Memlinc was
in Rogier's workshop when this triptych was made for the Milan duke.

We must intensify our search for dated or at least datable works by
Memlinc from his earliest period. Unfortunately the few inscribed dates
do not go back further than 1475.

The Floreins altarpiece in the Bruges hospital dates from 1479. The 112
Man of Sorrows, privately owned in France,[2] a replica of a panel at
Granada, is dated (genuinely I believe) 1475. The Danzig altarpiece was
done before the year 1473. Painted, as A. Warburg has demonstrated, for
Jacopo Tani, the altarpiece was to have been sent by sea route from
Bruges to Florence but was seized in 1473 by the Danzigers. That is to
say a *terminus ante quem* is firmly established. But I think that a simple
consideration can help us to date the altarpiece even more precisely. If
the Florentine donor had the large altarpiece shipped to Florence in 1473,
then it was from the outset intended to be set up in Florence and it is
unlikely that it remained many years at Bruges before being sent there.
We are therefore justified in dating it shortly before or around 1470.

---

*[1] The version from the French private collection is now in the National Gallery of Victoria,
Melbourne.
*[2] Now in Melbourne, see previous note.

Two other recognized works by the master take us back still further.

120   1468 is probably the correct date for the portrait at Antwerp of Forzore Spinelli, a Florentine medallist who in that year was in the service of Charles the Bold.[1]

110   The altarpiece with the *Virgin and Saints* belonging to the Duke of Devonshire,[2] which was donated by the Englishman John Donne, also dates from 1468. The argument in favour of this dating has already been indicated. Strictly speaking, however, none of these bring us early works. In 1468 Memlinc's style was already fully developed. At that time he was presumably in his thirties.

By nature Memlinc was an assured pictorial interpreter of quiet mood, at his best when presenting the Virgin in a circle of female saints or as a portraitist. In such tasks he seems, comparatively speaking, independent. This already applies to the Devonshire triptych, the early style of which is betrayed mainly by the thin, anaemic and dull treatment. Where dramatic force, vigorous movement, complex composition or a richer imaginative faculty are required the master remains until his late period dependent on Rogier, falls back on memories of his apprentice days. We note, not without some surprise, that the Christ in the *Last Judgment*, that is the central figure in the Danzig altarpiece, is a painfully exact copy of Rogier's figure in the Beaune altarpiece.

In his relationship to Memlinc, Hugo van der Goes was more a contemporary rival than a teacher. He was at Bruges for the wedding of Charles the Bold in 1468 when he did decorative paintings. Perhaps it was then that he came in contact with Tommaso Portinari, who was living at Bruges. The Italian patron of the Ghent painter, who commissioned the altarpiece in Florence, was at the same time a patron of Memlinc. We possess three portraits of Portinari by Memlinc (the single portrait in

104   the Altman collection, now in the Metropolitan Museum, New York,

113   the donor portrait in the Passion panel at Turin and the portrait in the Danzig altarpiece, where Tommaso appears as the man on St. Michael's scales).

Memlinc painted a diptych in which, in half-length figures, the *Descent*

106–107 *from the Cross* is spread over both halves of the picture. The two parts are in the Capilla Real at Granada. A copy or workshop replica of the right half with the *Mourning Women and St. John* can be seen in the Munich

---

*[1] The earlier identification with Forzore Spinelli was proved to be wrong by G. Hulin de Loo (in *Festschrift für Max J. Friedländer zum 60. Geburtstag*, 1927, pp. 103 ff.), who thought that the sitter was the medallist Giovanni Candida. Friedländer himself (*Die Altniederländische Malerei*, VI, 1928, p. 42) pointed out that the portrait represents a collector of coins rather than a medallist.

*[2] Now in the National Gallery, London.

Pinakothek. The original disposition of the scene is shown in a feeble imitation at Genoa. Here a clumsy compiler has turned the diptych into a triptych and added donor figures.

In a private collection in St. Petersburg I found a replica by Memlinc's own hand of the left half,[1] showing the body of Christ supported by three men, unfortunately not in perfect condition. It gives a slight variation in composition which agrees even better than does the version in Granada with the Genoa copy. Naturally the St. Petersburg panel also had on the right the group of mourning women.

The dramatically concentrated composition of this double panel is not in keeping with Memlinc's manner. It so happens that there is in the Berlin gallery a painting on canvas, seemingly fragmentary, which is Goes-like in the formal treatment, a group of *Mourning Women* which corresponds in its main features to the right wing of the Memlinc diptych. Thanks to Grete Ring's happy idea we can now complete the Berlin fragment by a Goes-like *Descent from the Cross*, of which replicas have been found at Altenburg and in the Bargello, Florence.[2]

The relationship between the Goes and the Memlinc compositions is evident and it is certain that the Ghent master was the giver. This relationship may be conceived as a brief encounter and an episode.

When studying Memlinc compositions we occasionally come upon motifs which seem to derive from Rogier's workshop but cannot be traced in the now existing stock of works. In dramatically dynamic groupings the Bruges master uses certain motifs inconsistently and with all the hall marks of derivation. In the centre panel of the altarpiece (the wings of which were destroyed by fire) in the von Kaufmann Collection,[3] the left arm of the dead Christ is not convincing, not conditioned by its position. If we assume the existence of a model in which the Madonna, more closely, more passionately united with the dead Christ, had pushed her arm beneath His left arm, enfolding His body, then we can understand the position of the arm. The case shows that Memlinc modified the severity of Rogier's forms to suit his even, decorous manner whereby he became involved in dangerous half-measures.

[1] Now in the D. Sickels Collection, New York. A panel with the *Mourning Women* in the Museum of São Paulo, Brazil, is probably the right wing of this diptych.

[2] The Berlin canvas is now recognized by Friedländer as an original by Hugo van der Goes (see *Die Altniederländische Malerei*, IV, 1926, p. 39). The other part of the original canvas, with the *Descent from the Cross*, was discovered in a private collection in Paris and published by Friedländer in *Oud Holland*, LXV, 1950, p. 150 ff.

[3] The centre panel, later in the Van Beuningen Collection, Vierhouten, was acquired in 1958 by the Museum Boymans-Van Beuningen, Rotterdam. In 1957 the damaged wings were in a private collection in Bruges.

96–97

Although Memlinc adopted thematic and compositional motifs, even such as were uncongenial to him, the form was consistently inspired by his personal feeling and regulated by an ever serene and unruffled sense of grace and moderation. We should expect a slow, undisturbed and organic development of his formal style and we can demonstrate this, though not without difficulty. Memlinc's attitude to nature is not that of a passionate wooer. He neither abandons himself to her nor does he tyrannize her. He observes and absorbs a certain amount—no more than Rogier—and moulds it with a gentle but firm hand.

The schematism, if there is any, of his formal idiom is unobtrusive. Certain constant characteristics, such as the rendering of the skin texture in the hands by means of fine parallel lines of light that proceed at right angles to the direction of the fingers, adapt themselves quietly to the whole.

Every attempt to formulate our impressions of Memlinc's compositional style leads to negative definitions. But it is just this lack of conspicuous qualities that is typical for his nature. Memlinc's portraits, of which an exceptionally large number survive, seem to have appealed to his contemporaries, especially the Italians living at Bruges. Memlinc was clearly the favoured portraitist of the wealthy business circles, he possessed something of the qualities that Van Dyck and Gainsborough, and society portrait painters of all ages, have used to increase their successes. Not that the intention of flattering his sitters influenced his art in any way, but his innate formal and intellectual sense toned down what was offensive and produced everywhere an agreeable likeness into which he infused something of his own pure and serene nature.

A searching examination reveals his portraits as more individual than a superficial inspection would suggest. The careful elucidating description of character is not obtrusive whilst habit and the professional practice of portrait painting envelop the personalities represented with a veil of uniformity. The main lines are selected and defined with flexible, pure and subtle draughtsmanship. The chance play of light is eliminated, abrupt and striking contrasts avoided. A gentle, slow, even and full projection of form is achieved more by wise manipulation of the line than by strong shadows. The hair, generally framing the head in luxuriant growth, is carefully portrayed in its material texture. Particularly near the edges, outside as well as inside, on the forehead and on the temples its loose and curly structure is richly and fully developed in sinuous strands and single threads.

Memlinc's faith is completely trusting, serenely confident, with no trace of fanaticism, melancholy or sentimentality, no feelings of guilt, no doubts, yearnings or driving ambition. His serene eye never penetrated to the dark depths where primitive passions are unleashed. His *Martyrdoms* 114, 115 thus seem to contain more of beatitude than of pain, and evil-doers go about their work without malice, even without real enthusiasm.

Of the famous Netherlanders of the fifteenth century Memlinc least deserves the title of innovator or expander in the realm of art. Neither through imagination nor through observation was he, like Goes or Geertgen, carried forward along the highway or even down byways. Compared with older masters he is imitative and his pictures seem faded in their cool opaque colouring.

If his popularity surpassed even that of Van Eyck, this unjust preference derived from a period that was sadly lacking in knowledge and understanding of early Netherlandish art. At that time, when the art of the fifteenth century in general, and Netherlandish art in particular, was felt as a contradiction to the norm of beauty, Memlinc was the first Netherlander to get past the barrier of aesthetic prejudice. Today when we use a different standard, Memlinc's position in the historical chain has been shifted. But over and above all change of taste his lovable and harmonious nature will ever continue to gain him friends.

GERARD DAVID

GERARD DAVID, who was the first in Bruges after Memlinc's death, has been rediscovered by recent research. He had been forgotten for centuries. Carel van Mander only says: "In olden times there was a certain Gerard of Bruges of whom I know no more than that Pieter Pourbus was heard to praise him highly as an excellent painter." The 'discovery' of this painter is a fine example of the successful collaboration between style criticism and documentary research, which marched independently but struck in unison. We owe the documentary evidence almost exclusively to James Weale, who since 1863 has been publishing material extracted from the Bruges archives. We owe its stylistic compilation to other experts. Finally, in his book published in 1905 (by Bruckmann in Munich), Von Bodenhausen successfully and with discerning insight combined the results. The master's *oeuvre* now comprises more than fifty items.

127

1460 (approx.)	Gerard, the son of Jan David, was born at Oudewater in Southern Holland. In the Rouen panel, painted in 1509, his self-portrait has been detected. He looks about fifty, which gives an approximate date for his birth.
1483	His name is first mentioned at Bruges.
1484	On January 14, Master in the St. Luke guild, Bruges.
1488–98	Commissions for the city of Bruges.
1488–1501	Honorary offices in the guild.
1496	Married Cornelia Cnoop, the daughter of a distinguished goldsmith.
1509	Altar panel for the Carmelite nuns, the picture that is now in the museum at Rouen.
1515	Stay at Antwerp (at least there is an entry referring to a Gerard of Bruges who is generally identified with David).
1523	Died on August 13.

The early and the late periods are problematical. David's compositions were widely copied at Bruges. The uninventive art of this town was long in shaking off the types he had invented. The painter whom we used to call Mostaert, and now call Adriaen Ysenbrandt, and Ambrosius Benson often seem to be imitators of David, whose influence on Bruges book illumination was immense. David's activity flows over into that of his pupils, the boundary lines are hard to define.

No less difficult is the task for the art critic attempting to clarify the growth of his style, its early origins and relationship to Dutch tradition. What did David bring with him when he came to the town of Jan van Eyck and Memlinc?

Four established major works give an all-round idea of the master's ability, temperament and sensibility. They date from his middle period (between 1498 and 1509).

1. The two Judgment panels with the *Verdict of Cambyses* and the 126 *Flaying of Sisamnes* painted for the town hall at Bruges, now in the Communal Museum there. The first panel is dated 1498. That very year David received payment for a painting that he had completed for the jurors' room.

2. *Canon Bernardino de Salviatis and three Saints* now in the National 125 Gallery, London, probably painted for the church of St. Donatian, Bruges, shortly after 1501.

3. The altarpiece with the *Baptism of Christ*, donated by Jan de 131 Trompes, who is shown on the wings with his two wives, in the Communal Museum, Bruges. Since Elizabeth van der Meersch, the first wife, appears in the usual place on the inner wing opposite the donor, the altarpiece was probably commissioned before 1502 (the year of her death). In that case, however, the outer wings, where the second wife with her four-year-old daughter is represented in an unusual place, must have been added around 1508.

4. *The Virgin in a circle of female Saints*, now in the Rouen museum, 127 painted for the Carmelite Convent of Sion at Bruges, donated by the painter, whose self-portrait can be seen on the extreme left. The date 1509 authenticated from documents.

To these a long series of stylistically related works in David's mature style can be added.

When the task requires no more than a grouping of holy and devout women, David's compositions make a solemn though monotonous impression. No urgency, no profane gestures upset the dignified attitudes of the well-formed but not coquettish women and maidens, in whom soul and body, eye and figure are all similarly conceived and directed. The sumptuous splendour, the beautifully shaped hands with their solemn gestures, the heavy materials with the few simple drapery motifs, the symmetrical clarity of the groups, the gravity and calm collectedness, everything suggests a religious ceremony, a familiarity with church ritual. Through the conscientious leisureliness of the outline and modelling of the forms many things acquire statuesque-like isolation, everything is oppressed and rigidly banned. The compositions never even begin to flow. The *Judgment* panels give us the measure of his talent. The execution of the guilty judge is observed with pedantic accuracy like a surgical operation.

In the Louvre is a triptych of the *Virgin*, that came from the Garriga sale, which I claimed years ago for Gerard David. The attribution seems on the whole to have been favourably received and was accepted in von Bodenhausen's book, although in the Louvre it is still among the anonymous works.[1] The donor was Jan de Sedano, for whom, at least ten years 128 later, David executed the *Marriage at Cana*, also in the Louvre. Whereas the *Marriage* reveals the fully mature familiar Davidian style, the style in the Triptych of the Virgin, on the wings of which the donor pair seem considerably younger, is a curious blend of tenderness, serenity, meagreness and constraint. The figures stand firmly, rise and take shape pillar-like in their sheer terseness. The modelling intent on sculptural, even statuesque forms remains characteristic for the master but the perceptive faculty grows heavier and duller. The age of the donor and in particular the date of his marriage would have supplied the best means of dating the work. But in default of these dates we can judge the period from the costume of the donatrix. This form of coif does not seem to have been worn after 1490. And the general stylistic effect confirms such a dating.

In the attitude of the Christ Child there is a connection with the famous *Paele Madonna* by Jan van Eyck. Two variants of the figure of the Virgin in the triptych are known from David's workshop, one at Darmstadt and one in the Johnson Collection, Philadelphia. Strangely enough from these replicas two threads, different threads, lead to Van Eyck. In Darmstadt, namely, angels making music have been added which are freely copied from the celebrated angels of the Ghent altarpiece whilst in the Philadelphia replica the carpet is exactly modelled on the Eyckian carpet in the *Paele Madonna*. The decorative motif of the nude children holding garlands links the Garriga triptych to Memlinc. As far as I know, Memlinc used this motif three times. David, who was

*[1] Now catalogued in the Louvre as by Gerard David.

uninventive in such things, made use of this Renaissance motif, perhaps
the first of its kind in Netherlandish painting, not only in the triptych of
the Virgin but also in one of the *Judgment* panels of 1498, in the second,
as I believe later case, however, he gave the children above a better and
more secure place on a console. With Memlinc, and also in David's first
use of the motif, the children are stuck uncomfortably on the arch.

A relationship to Rogier van der Weyden is shown in the half-figure of
the suckling Madonna belonging to Mr. Traumann, Madrid.[1] Judging by
the style, we have here a fine work by David of about 1495. The composition however is not by him. Nearly a dozen replicas of this composition
are known, some by inferior hands, some more archaic than David's
version. A few of these replicas are obviously copied from Rogier, who
seems to have established the standard form, though Rogier's original
version appears to be lost. The imprint of his manner, however, can
still be felt even in David's work—apart from the landscape, which is
purely Davidian. In an article in the *Jahrbuch der preussischen Kunstsammlungen*, 1906, and in an older article in the same periodical, I pointed out
an even more interesting relationship between David and Hugo van der
Goes.

There is in the Pinakothek in Munich an *Adoration of the Magi*, a horizontal picture with a many-figured composition, that has given rise to
much speculation. To those who concentrated on the individual details,
such as the hands of the eldest king, David's authorship seemed certain.
Experts of the rank of Scheibler have long regarded this panel as a work
by David. On the other hand all experts were agreed that the movement
was too lively, the composition alien, too rich in invention, too involved,
too dramatic. It so happens that in the Kaiser Friedrich Museum, Berlin,
there is a far weaker version of almost the same composition, and this
Berlin copy shows so clearly, though in slight distortion, the characteristics of Goes's art that the solution of the riddle is as follows: David
copied the Munich picture from a work of the Ghent master now lost.
Incidentally the head of the Virgin has been spoilt by a restorer. These
pieces of evidence round off our idea of David's art. We note a quality
of dependence. We see that the Bruges master copied, whom he copied
and how he copied. And thereby his personal style emerges all the more
clearly.

Unlike his contemporary and fellow countryman Geertgen of Haarlem,
David left home early and at Bruges sought successfully to link up with the
great tradition. What he lost in originality, through eclectic endeavour,

*[1] Now in the Museo Lázaro Galdiano, Madrid.

he gained in culture and understanding. The convention of the church picture supplied the framework for the successful development of gifts that from the outset were probably less potentially progressive than the talent of Geertgen.

It would be difficult to find a single early Netherlandish devotional picture of such sonorous accord, such gravity and such firm structure as 132 David's *Madonna with three female Saints and a donor* in the National Gallery, London (formerly Lyne Stephens Collection).

The simple composition is relatively loose, not tied symmetrically, the space clearly articulated. The horizontal aspect of the floor provides a solid foundation for the full and plastic figures rising up freely in space. The drapery lines are grand and stately. The uniform, almost sad expression knits the whole firmly together. Two hands, in masterly foreshortening, one reaching inwards, one forwards, heighten the spatial effect. In the detailed execution David almost attains Jan van Eyck's standard. Typical for the rather weary heads, so delicately individualized, are the low but firmly out-thrust chins, the high broad foreheads, the slanting eyes. Admittedly, this panel is a culminating point, perhaps even an exception, in the unity of the lighting, the warm colouring and the fully developed chiaroscuro. Generally David's panels seem more sober, attuned to a cooler key, the composition, with the heads adjusted to the same height, all too clear and all too regular.

David was no determined innovator but rather a guardian of tradition who represented at the eleventh hour the art of the fifteenth century in conservative Bruges, whilst in rising Antwerp Quentin Massys, probably an exact contemporary, was practising the differently oriented art of the new era.

GEERTGEN TOT SINT JANS

ALMOST all the early altar painting in Holland has been destroyed so that, as far as our limited knowledge goes, Geertgen tot Sint Jans becomes the representative of the fifteenth century. He worked at Haarlem, and does not seem to have left Holland but apparently was not entirely unaffected by the art of the Flemish towns.[1] His very real originality must be regarded in the first place as a personal quality, then— though with caution—as national Dutch. Though the discovery of the one work by Ouwater, the *Raising of Lazarus* (Berlin) unfortunately bore 86 no further fruits it has been possible from our master's accredited chief work—the pictures in Vienna that formed the front and back of an 137–138 altarpiece wing clearly described by van Mander—to establish a considerable *oeuvre* for him and to gain a many-sided idea of his personality.

We have two *Madonnas*, one unusually large (Berlin, Kaiser-Friedrich Museum) one unusually small (Milan, Ambrosiana), no less than three *Adorations* (Amsterdam, Prague, Dutch private collection),[2] the charming diptych in Brunswick,[3] the *Raising of Lazarus* in the Louvre, the *St. John* 136 *in the Wilderness*, Berlin, the symbolic representation of the *Holy Kindred* in 142 Amsterdam, the problematic *View of a Church* in Haarlem—that gets us nowhere—the *Man of Sorrows* in Utrecht, the night scene of the 143 *Nativity* in the v. Onnes Collection, Holland,[4] and finally a not fully 139 accredited portrait, formerly in the Leuchtenberg Collection, St. Petersburg[5], which represents the second wife of the Duke of Cleves. These

[1] Calling attention to the borrowings by Geertgen from the Monforte *Adoration* by Hugo van der Goes, Friedländer later did not exclude the possibility of Geertgen's stay in Ghent (*Die Altniederländische Malerei*, V, 1927, p. 18). If, as suggested by R. Koch (in *The Art Bulletin* XXXIII, 1951, p. 259) the "Gheerkin de Hollandere" mentioned as an apprentice in the accounts of the Guild of St. John and St. Luke at Bruges in 1474–75 is identical with Geertgen tot Sint Jans, the latter must have spent at least part of his apprentice years in Flanders.

[2] Now in the O. Reinhart Collection, Winterthur.

[3] The Brunswick diptych is now generally excluded from Geertgen's *oeuvre*. In a detailed study of Geertgen and his circle, Friedländer has given this diptych to a Geertgen follower, to whom he was also able to attribute several other paintings (*Die Altniederländische Malerei*, VI, 1927, pp. 51 ff.). For the Master of the Brunswick Dyptych, see also p. 113, note 4.

[4] Now in the National Gallery, London.

[5] *Trésors d'Art en Russie*, 1904. *Two important additions to Geertgen's oeuvre published by 140, 141 Friedländer (in *Maandblad voor beeldende Kunsten*, XXV, 1949, p. 187, and XXVI, 1950, p. 10) are the *Virgin and Child* in the Museum Boymans-Van Beuningen, Rotterdam, and the *Adoration of the Kings* in the Cleveland museum. To these should now be added a *St. Jerome* in the P. & N. de Boer Stichting, Amsterdam. The Rotterdam picture has been identified as the part of a diptych, the

thirteen works were done at approximately the same time. If van Mander is perhaps mistaken in allotting the master only twenty-eight years, he does in fact seem to have died young. None of the paintings listed here seems to have been done considerably before or appreciably after 1490. The differences between one or other of the links in the chain, however great they may appear to be, can be partly explained by the influence of the subject, the condition of the picture and the size.

Next to Hugo van der Goes, Geertgen is the Netherlandish artist in the second half of the fifteenth century with the greatest claim to creativeness and originality. The difficulty in assessing his achievement is all the greater because it is not easy to rid our minds of all that came later. Geertgen was probably born about the same time as Gerard David—1465—and probably died about the same time as Memlinc—1495. Our immediate reaction to the Vienna panels, a feeling of excitement at their purposeful boldness, is increased rather than weakened by a more intensive study of all we possess of the master, for we become aware of the flexibility with which his perception of nature was ever adapted to the task before him.

138   In the *Lamentation over Christ* in Vienna, the mourners and the body of Christ in their plastic and spatial arrangement are resolutely adjusted to the seemingly horizontal surface of the ground. There is the illusion of a cubic bulk graduated to correspond with the recession, which convinces at every distance from the eye. The artistic means, without which this effect could never have been achieved, is the incisively sharp contrast of light and shade in the foreground figures, a contrast studied in the studio and not out-of-doors. The antithesis of the light values becomes less emphatic in proportion to the smallness of Geertgen's pictures. The small panels lack the tautness, lack the bursting rotundity or prismatic faceting, the deep rents and the jaggedness that is characteristic for the foreground shapes on the large Vienna panels.

The landscape is surprising in the soft succulent green of the vegetation. To grasp the significance of Geertgen's achievement we need only recall the position of landscape within the general run of early Netherlandish painting. The landscape setting is represented in natural relationship to the figures. Elements widely discrepant elsewhere here seem fused to organic unity.

The landscape cannot be ignored without destroying meaning and essence of the whole. The primitive device of the 'three grounds' is done

other wing of which, a *Crucifixion with St. Jerome*, is in the National Gallery of Scotland, Edinburgh, see I. Q. van Regteren Altena (in *Oud-Holland*, LXXXI, 1966, pp. 76 ff.). His doubts as to the autograph character of the diptych are certainly justified for the Edinburgh panel.

away with. Geertgen's contemporaries evoke the illusion of depth with masses like stage sets and stacked hills or trees parallel to the picture plane, the backgrounds alone being richly developed; they suggest distance in the landscape by the expedient of a division the inadequacy of which is generally betrayed in the middle ground. In Geertgen's pictures the grounds flow imperceptibly into one another. His landscape unfolds luxuriously in the middle ground. He achieves the illusion of distance without resorting to the 'prospect', the distant view, the wide horizon. The surrounding vegetation takes over the function of architecture and makes as important a contribution as the figures to the general effect. Geertgen's lyricism lies very largely in his landscape.

We like to feel that there is some deep-rooted cause underlying this blossoming of landscape representation at Haarlem, the town where Ruysdael worked, and eagerly seize on van Mander's passage: "Of the earliest painters it is affirmed and assured that it was Haarlem where in olden days the best and earliest manner of landscape representation arose."

Just as Geertgen with obstinate determination fashions figures that rise freely in space and stand firmly with their soles on the ground so he avoids strong protrusions and, like a sculptor in stone, binds the body masses together with austerely pure, sometimes almost mathematical outlines. His profiles are dull, the eyes shallow, the noses seem short, slightly arched and uptilted. The concrete observation leads the master unhesitatingly to introduce genre, even burlesque motifs and gives holy and profane alike an earthy solidity. Far removed from affectation and sentimentality he pursues the expression with naive objectivity to the verge of the comic. His composition is not painterly in as far as it is anything but surface decoration, and nowhere veils or blurs the form, and not graphic in as far as the boundaries never appear firmly stressed. Light is never sovereign but rather subsidiary, as is also the colour, which, at times exquisitely harmonious, at times glowing in splendour, always remains subordinate. He did not aspire to chiaroscuro in the sense of the later Dutch painters but with clear and consistent observation of the conditions of light, the inner and cast shadows, he created the basis on which the later art of Dutch painting could arise.

JEROME BOSCH

WHAT rather than how, content rather than form, these are the problems that absorb the art lover when first encountering the phenomenon of Jerome Bosch—to the extent that, generally speaking, no proper distinction is drawn between the original on the one hand and copies or imitations on the other. The invention is admired but little attention is paid to the manner of drawing and painting. The only serious attempt to comprehend Bosch's art, the article published by Dollmayr in 1898,[1] was as successful as a guide through an unfamiliar world of ideas as it was misguided in the stylistic criticism.

Bosch, whatever else he may have been, was certainly a great and original artist so that mind and matter form an entity in his work and in his imagination idea and image are conceived simultaneously. Therefore the study of form will give us just as much insight into his world of ideas as the understanding of his intellectual outlook will aid the work of stylistic criticism. We have not yet arrived at the deplorable period which suffered from the dualism: *unus invenit, alter fecit*. And if diligent engravers of the sixteenth century multiplied compositions by Bosch, the master himself never worked mechanically—he worked creatively.

In many of the surviving works by Bosch even the subjects are peculiar to him as, for instance, the abstruse *Temptations* or the allegories of the Last Things, others are common property as regards the subject-matter but are re-interpreted and interwoven with original motifs and a luxurious welter of ideas.

Two methods suggest themselves to clarify Bosch's manner. We can either, as Justi and Dollmayr attempted in masterly descriptions, concentrate on representations that in content and execution are peculiar to the master or else we can study Bosch's approach to a subject often successfully treated by his contemporaries and fellow countrymen, e.g. the familiar subject of the *Adoration of the Kings*. In this way Bosch's attitude to convention is revealed.

The subject of the Epiphany in itself was anything but suitable to bring the master's imagination to exploding point. We possess at least three versions by his hand:

[1] In the Vienna *Jahrbuch der Kunsthistorischen Sammlungen*.

IV–V. Bosch: *Adam and Eve; Hell*. Wings of the 'Hay-Wain', Escorial

(*a*) The panel from the Lippmann Collection (now Metropolitan Museum, New York),

(*b*) the panel from the sale of the Earl of Ellenborough (now Johnson 147 Collection, Philadelphia),

(*c*) the celebrated, oft-copied triptych in the Prado.   148–150

Constrained by the commission Bosch curbed his instincts, particularly in the Madrid altarpiece, where the donor and donatrix with saints appear on the wings. All the more confidently, therefore, can we interpret the deviations from the norm as the exigencies of his temperament.

The biography of Bosch is not known exactly. The master, who died in 1516, seems to have been born around 1450. He is shown as a man well advanced in years on a portrait engraving which, however, must not be regarded as an absolutely reliable document. His name occurs in Hertogenbosch documents between 1493[1] and 1512.

This town, the centre of the master's activity, where in all probability despite his name 'van Aken'[2] he was born, lies within the boundaries of present-day Holland in Northern Brabant, far from Haarlem, the artistic centre of Holland proper. We know next to nothing of the art practised in this area and it seems hardly possible to find an historical basis for Bosch's art, whilst the tradition deriving from him is mainly in evidence at Antwerp (though, admittedly, that city was the centre of attraction at the beginning of the sixteenth century).

Of his known contemporaries the so-called Master of the Virgo inter 133 Virgines, whom I have attempted to locate at Delft, comes closest to him, but not really close. The costumes in his pictures afford some aid for the dating. The Prado triptych may have been done about 1490. An *Adoration of the Kings* has probably survived by every artist who worked between 1470 and 1500. There is thus a wide choice for comparative study.

The standpoint of the painter can be fixed from the proportions of the figures to the picture surface. The human figure is as far removed from Bosch's interest as from his eye. Its weight, cubic bulk and individual details are in themselves of indifference to him and he makes not the slightest attempt to produce the illusion of reality by a painstaking study of models. In his compositions the figure has value only as an expressive contour and as a link in the narrative chain.

[1] As later research has established, it is in 1480/81 that Bosch appears for the first time in the registers of the Brotherhood of the Holy Virgin at Hertogenbosch (under the name 'Jeroen the painter').

[2] Hertogenbosch citizens with the name 'Van Aken' can be traced back to 1399, as recently stressed again by L. von Baldass, *Hieronymus Bosch*, London 1960, p. 9.

The people stand like accessories in front of the landscape, not really within the landscape space, not surrounded by air. And yet he had a vision of that unity of figure and landscape that Pieter Bruegel was to realize. Bosch's large but geographically visualized landscapes have a very high horizon and seem to be surveyed from a tower, the figures on the other hand have their own much lower-lying horizon, are upright and seen without foreshortening. No proper illusion of depth can result from such an archaic division and dualism of perspective construction. And in fact the emphasis does seem to be on the surface decoration in Bosch's pictures, although breadth and distance in the landscape backgrounds are carefully expressed in line and colour. A vital factor for the illusion of space, the middle ground, is lacking.

The emotional content of the *Adoration of the Kings*, the dignified and humble reverence before the Christ Child, is merely incidental in Bosch's treatment. Instead of driving straight to the core of the theme, the subject under his hand bristles with adventurous and picturesque elements extracted from the bible story. His power of observation, subordinated as it is to an exuberant imagination, is concentrated less on the actual text than on the marginal trimmings. The Virgin with the Christ Child do not impress themselves on our minds. On the other hand the tumble-down hut, the Moorish king and the inquisitive shepherds are the motifs that he delights in elaborating. The court figures and the chorus are vivid and convincing but the protagonists seem insipid and indifferent. Dignity and holiness are expressed in beautifully developed forms but the terse and cursory language shows little imprint of the master's personality and seems strangely archaic. On the other hand abnormality and deformity stimulate Bosch to personal interpretation. With an aversion for architecture, symmetry and regularity he combines a diabolic delight in the apparent anarchy of organic form. Surprising form interests him, normal form leaves him cold.

As a psychologist Bosch is one-sided to the point of monomania. The very idea of the Passion of Christ evokes in his mind an orgy of mockery 155–157 and devilish spite and he cannot invent enough hideous monstrosities to pour down hatred and contempt on the adversaries of Our Lord, whereas the divine suffering seems vague or even ambiguous.

In his observation of human nature Bosch is certainly a precursor of Pieter Bruegel but his sense of reality is deflected, oppressed and haunted by visions, by the excrescences of an inhuman imagination that distorts the natural.

Like so many of the best masters of Germanic origin Bosch has all the makings of an illustrator. In actual fact, however, as far as we know he never had occasion to do proper illustrations, but everywhere in his work the narrative overflows the boundaries of panel painting and is often unintelligible because the explanatory text is lacking.

Bosch has all the makings of a landscape painter. There is character and grandeur in his wide and barren plains. Perhaps he is more entitled than Patenier, a professional landscape painter, to be included among the pioneers and innovators in this field.

However progressive in his intellectual independence and robust inventiveness the master may be, his formal idiom and manner of painting are still of the fifteenth century. By studying his terse sharp lines in their archaic ductus and the glazed clarity of the thinly applied paint (in well-preserved originals) we can avoid confusing his works with those of his imitators.

Primitive even in the circle of his contemporaries, Bosch composes like a carver in relief or a medallist; his profiled figures are thin, almost transparent, everything is flattened onto the surface. The essentials are expressed in decoratively attractive silhouettes. The figures lack the leaden heaviness with which the fifteenth-century Netherlanders weighed them down by intensive study of nature and careful modelling. A rapid smooth-flowing line, precisely directed, gives an ethereal quality to his pictures.

Meagre limbs, thin sticks, branches, slender tree trunks all attract him; keen-edged, prickly, cactus-like forms infuse an uncanny life into the surface. Dots and lines in sharp staccato strokes, broad, pearly or ridgy, preferably light on a dark surface, produce a tingling sensation. In this way foliage is expressed in bright dots on dark surfaces. A harmonious cool colouring, glistening opal-like and transparent, particularly in the bright patches, does more to enhance the decorative charm than to increase the realistic effect.

The basic forms of the human figure, which is graceful and flexible in effect, are surely grasped but superficial intimations suffice him for the details. We can expect little reverence for nature from one who tries to poach on the Creator.

In his fantastic imagination Bosch defies the laws of nature, ignores the barriers between man and beast, between human works and the work of nature. Everything ever conceived in popular superstition and all the terror of Hell become visible in freaks and monsters. And he succeeds in giving these impossible creatures a certain credibility of appearance and movement.

Bosch is no portrait painter. He and Pieter Bruegel are among the few early Netherlandish painters by whom no portraits survive. Not the individual thing in itself but only individual abnormalities, excessive individuality, caricature have any meaning for him. The donor portraits 148–149 in the Prado are weak. The donatrix looks like St. Agnes's sister. A clear distinction is usually drawn between the saint and the donor portrait but here they flow into one another.

Bosch's human beings have thin, pale, elderly faces and generally participate in some sly feeble cunning. The pure and holy often have a foolish smile whilst evil lurks everywhere awaiting an opportunity to erupt.

Bosch's drapery folds seem flattened out, more linear than plastically conceived. The lines are not stiff or wide-sweeping, not crumpled or bunched up but rather finely designed with a well-controlled clarity of movement. At times widely arching lines predominate, as for instance in 147 the *Adoration of Kings*, Philadelphia, or again straight and angular ones 159 meet as in the *St. John on Patmos* in Berlin, I suspect that the curving drapery folds belong to an earlier, the straight ones to a later period. But owing to the lack of authentically dated pieces the chronological order of Bosch's work is still uncertain, despite recent research.

Our stock of Bosch paintings, even after a critical rejection of the many copies and imitations, remains considerably larger than Dollmayr assumed. Dollmayr rightly rejected some works from Justi's list, for instance the triptych at Valencia, but was wrong in discarding several others. A number of genuine works were unknown both to Justi and Dollmayr. Cohen's list in Thieme-Becker's *Künstlerlexikon* is fairly complete.[1] Lafond's richly illustrated book on Bosch is quite worthless because it lacks any critical approach.

In my attempt at classification I intend to ignore the chronology and arrange the material by subjects, because in this way the compositionally and stylistically related works can be put together, which facilitates the general survey.

I have already mentioned the three panels of the *Adoration of the Kings* —full-length figures staged against wide landscape backgrounds. Bosch liked to represent the Life of Christ—preferably the horror scenes of the Passion—in half-length figures which enabled him to give a maximum of expression in terrifying caricatures to the relatively large heads of the enemies of Christ and to the executioners.

---

*[1] Friedländer himself published more complete lists in *Die Altniederländische Malerei*, V, 1927, pp. 143 ff. and XIV, 1937, pp. 100 ff.

The *Nativity of Christ* in half-length figures, Cologne museum, which was accepted by Justi, is probably only a copy of the mid-sixteenth century (like the corresponding generally rejected version in the Brussels gallery). Two small altar-wings from a *Nativity of Christ* on the Munich art market, not known to me, have passed to the Johnson Collection, Philadelphia. On one of the wings are royal horsemen—similar to those on the central panel of the *Hay-Wain* in the Escorial—the kings with their retinues; the other wing shows the shepherds. Of the Passion scenes with half-length figures the *Crowning with Thorns* in the Escorial is genuine[1]. Not one of the variations of this composition (Antwerp museum, formerly Kaufmann Collection, Berlin, and elsewhere) is an original. On the other hand *Christ carrying the Cross* in the Ghent museum is genuine; it is re- 156 markable for the densely packed mass of horrible hate-distorted heads with which, heedless of natural spatial effect, Bosch has filled the entire picture plane. *Christ before Pilate* in the Art Museum, Princeton, is similar in conception and composition.

Among the Passion scenes with full-length figures *Christ carrying the Cross* in the Escorial should be accepted—it is comparatively mild in expression and relief-like in treatment throughout. Further there is an *Ecce Homo* in the Staedel Institute, Frankfurt. Far more original in inven- tion is an *Ecce Homo*, arranged in two rows one above the other, in the 155 Johnson Collection, Philadelphia.

Several years ago I saw a *Crucifixion of Christ*, not mentioned anywhere, 146 on the Brussels art market, a composition with no personal characteristics.[2] The Rogier pattern still lingers particularly in the figure of Christ on the Cross. The subject did not permit the artist to give free rein to his inven- tive faculties. On the left next to the Cross the Virgin and St. John stand quietly together, on the right a youthful donor kneels, with St. Peter as his patron. The landscape is characteristic, with barren middle- ground and richly silhouetted background.

For Bosch a saint is first and foremost a being who is tempted, attacked and derided by devils. The famous oft-copied *Temptation of St. Anthony*, 153 an altarpiece with wings, is in Portugal. Single panels with St. Anthony can be seen in the Prado and in Berlin. In the perfectly preserved picture in Madrid the saint is seated huddled in the foreground gazing into space and lost in visions whilst the forces of Hell advance with cunningly contrived weapons of war. Here, admittedly, as in the similar Berlin

*[1] In addition to this version, the *Crowning with Thorns* acquired by the National Gallery, 144 London, in 1934, has been accepted by Friedländer as autograph (in *Die Altniederländische Malerei*, XIV, 1937, p. 101).
*[2] Now in the Royal Museum, Brussels.

picture, the devilish creatures are so small in size that the attack seems more like the odium of noxious insects than threatening.

159 Even St. John, who sits writing on Patmos and looks upwards to see the vision of an angel and the Virgin in the heavens above—even he is not spared. Like a spy from hell, unnoticed by the Evangelist, a small devil is pressed against the rock. This panel, on the reverse side of which the whole Passion of Christ is represented in monochrome, done in one grand sweep, is in the Kaiser Friedrich Museum, Berlin.[1]

One of the two badly damaged triptychs in the Vienna museum has St. Jerome on the central panel and SS Aegidius and Anthony on the wings. The second Vienna triptych depicts the *Martyrdom of St. Julia*.[2] The

154 Ghent museum has recently acquired a panel with *St. Jerome* lying full-length on the ground, strangely impressive in his act of penitence. Here even the fauna and flora seem insidious so that devilish spooks appear to be lurking everywhere.

158 The roundel with the *Prodigal Son*, in the collection of Dr. Figdor, Vienna,[3] is genre-like in conception; it has been pertinently described by Glück.[4]

Of the *Operations for the Stone* the version in the Prado is an original (not the one in Amsterdam). To our minds there is in such productions a contradiction between the humour of the action and the terse solemn archaism of the drawing.

There is quite a volume of literature on the three many-figured capital

152, 151, works by Bosch in the Escorial: the two triptychs, *Hay-Wain* and *Garden*
145 *of Earthly Delights*, and the table-top with the *Deadly Sins*.[5] Justi gave exhaustive descriptions of these compositions.[6] A replica of the *Hay-Wain* has turned up at Aranjuez[7] (the wings are in the Prado and the Escorial), the quality of which is hardly lower than the version preserved in its entirety

152, IV in the Escorial. Of the representations of the *Last Judgment* the triptych in
–v the Vienna Academy is still most entitled to be accepted as genuine.

Four narrow panels, now rather dulled, in the Venice Academy, said to have come from the Doges' Palace, representing the Blessed and the Condemned from a Last Judgment, are originals.[8]

---

[1] Now in the Staatliche Museen, Berlin-Dahlem.
[2] Both Viennese triptychs are now in the Palazzo Ducale, Venice.
[3] Now in the Museum Boymans-van Beuningen, Rotterdam.
[4] *Jahrbuch der Preussischen Kunstsammlungen*, XXV.
[5] The *Garden of Earthly Delights* and the table top with the *Deadly Sins* are now in the Prado, Madrid.
[6] *Jahrbuch der Preussischen Kunstsammlungen*, X.
[7] Now in the Prado, Madrid.
[8] Two were published as School of Jerome Bosch by Dülberg, *Frühholländer in Italien*, Plates VIII, IX.

The *Garden of Earthly Delights* represents a culminating point. Here the insistent urge of the illustrator produced a heap of compositionally equal sections rather than a real composition.

In the images he creates Bosch remains a solitary figure in the fifteenth century. His conception of landscape seems to have borne fruit—in particular in Patenier and directly and indirectly also in others. Bosch was widely copied in the sixteenth century but the copyists were interested only in the subject-matter, in the entertainment, moralizing and horror values. The interest and the demand for these pictorial themes lasted until far into the sixteenth century, Jerome Cock in particular published prints after compositions by Bosch. And round about 1550 this publisher seems to have introduced Pieter Bruegel the elder to Bosch's art. Especially in his earlier period Bruegel sometimes appears to be an imitator and continuator of Bosch.

Until very recently there has been little understanding for the quality of original works by Bosch. What has survived is largely due to the taste of Philip II of Spain, who amassed in the Escorial everything by Bosch that he could lay hands on, similar to the way in which, at a later date, the Habsburg princes such as Rudolph II and Archduke Leopold Wilhelm sought the works of Pieter Bruegel.

THE PLATES

THE FIFTEENTH CENTURY

I. VAN EYCK: *God the Father*. Detail from the Ghent altarpiece (plate 2)

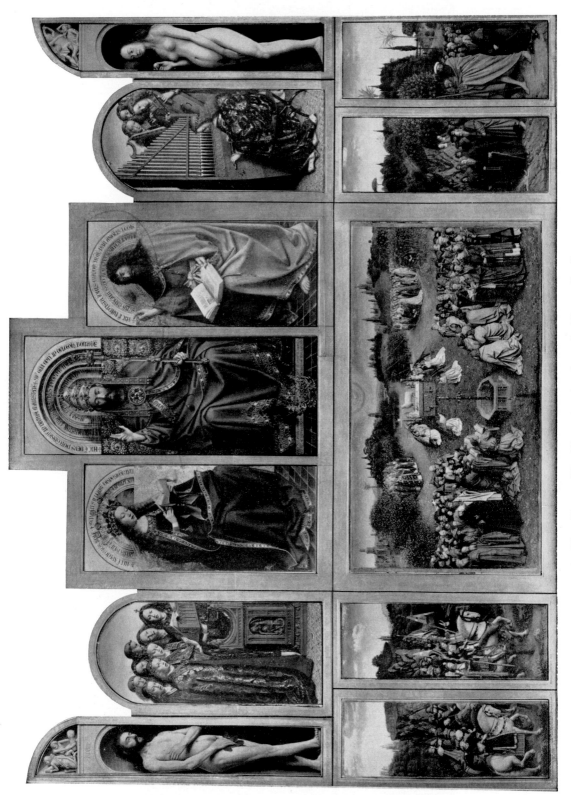

2. VAN EYCK: *The Ghent altarpiece* (open). Ghent, St. Bavo

3. VAN EYCK: *The Adoration of the Lamb.* Detail from plate 2

4. Van Eyck: *Singing Angels*. Detail from plate 2

5. VAN EYCK: *Angels making Music*. Detail from plate 2

6. Van Eyck: *Adam and Eve*. Detail from plate 2

7. VAN EYCK: *The Ghent altarpiece* (closed). Ghent, St. Bavo

8a. Van Eyck: *The Angel of the Annunciation*. In the lunette: *The Prophet Zechariah*.
Detail from plate 7

8b. Van Eyck: *The Virgin Annunciate*. In the lunette: *The Prophet Micah*.
Detail from plate 7

9. Van Eyck: *St. John the Baptist and St. John the Evangelist*. Detail from plate 7

10. VAN EYCK: *Jodocus Vyd* and *Isabella Borluut*. Detail from plate 7

11. JAN VAN EYCK: *The Three Marys at the Sepulchre*. Rotterdam, Museum Boymans-Van Beuningen

12. JAN VAN EYCK: *Virgin and Child with the Chancellor Rolin*. Paris, Louvre

13. JAN VAN EYCK: *The Virgin in the Church*. Berlin-Dahlem, Staatliche Museen

14. JAN VAN EYCK: *The Annunciation*.
Washington, National Gallery of Art (Mellon Collection)

15. JAN VAN EYCK: *Virgin and Child with St. Barbara, St. Elizabeth of Hungary and a Carthusian.* New York, Frick Collection

16. JAN VAN EYCK: *Virgin and Child with St. Donatian, St. George and Canon van der Paele. Bruges, Museum*

17. JAN VAN EYCK: '*Cardinal Niccolò Albergati*'. Vienna, Kunsthistorisches Museum

18. Jan van Eyck: *Margaret, the Painter's Wife*. Bruges, Museum

19. JAN VAN EYCK: *Virgin and Child*. Centre panel of a triptych. Dresden, Gallery

20. JAN VAN EYCK: *Giovanni Arnolfini and his Wife*. London, National Gallery

21. JAN VAN EYCK: *St. Barbara*. Brush drawing. Antwerp, Museum

e uentre matris mee uocauit me dñs
nomine meo. et posuit os meū sicut
gladium acutum subteğumento
manus sue protexit me posuit me

22. TURIN BOOK OF HOURS: *The Birth of St. John the Baptist*. Miniature. Turin, Museo Civico

23. TURIN BOOK OF HOURS: *The Voyage of St. Julian.* Miniature, destroyed by fire

24. JAN VAN EYCK: *The Stigmatization of St. Francis.*
Philadelphia, John G. Johnson Collection

25. Petrus Christus: *Edward Grimston*. London, National Gallery
On loan from the Earl of Verulam

26. PETRUS CHRISTUS: *A Young Lady*. Berlin-Dahlem, Staatliche Museen

27. Petrus Christus: *The Lamentation over Christ.* Brussels, Museum

28. PETRUS CHRISTUS: *The Lamentation over Christ*. New York, Metropolitan Museum of Art

29. **Petrus Christus**: *The Nativity*. Washington, National Gallery of Art (Mellon Collection)

30. Petrus Christus: *Virgin and Child with St. Barbara and a Carthusian*. Berlin-Dahlem, Staatliche Museen

31. Petrus Christus: *A Carthusian*. New York, Metropolitan Museum of Art

32. PETRUS CHRISTUS: *St. Eligius weighing the Wedding Rings of a Bridal Couple.*
New York, Robert Lehman Collection

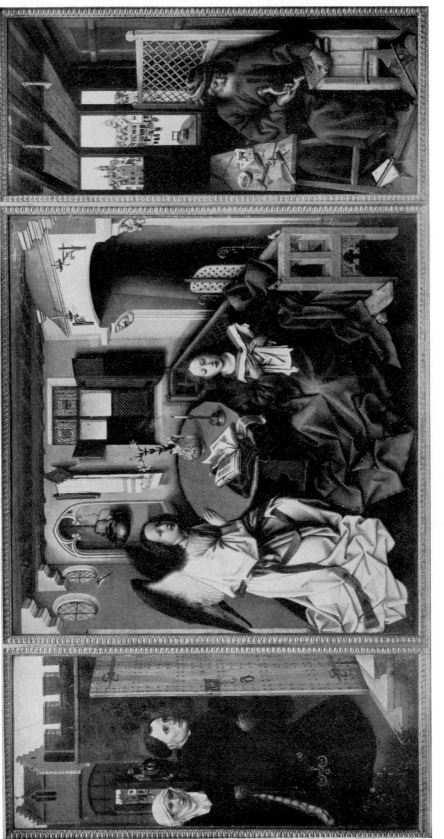

33. MASTER OF FLÉMALLE: *The Annunciation.* On the wings: *St. Joseph and two Donors.* Known as the Inghelbrecht altarpiece. New York, Metropolitan Museum of Art

34. MASTER OF FLÉMALLE: *The Betrothal of the Virgin.* Madrid, Prado

35. Master of Flémalle: *St. James the Greater and St. Clare*. Reverse of plate 34

36. Copy after the Master of Flémalle: *The Descent from the Cross*. Liverpool, Walker Art Gallery

37. MASTER OF FLÉMALLE: *Thief on the Cross*. Frankfurt, Staedel Institute

38. Master of Flémalle: *The Nativity*. Dijon, Museum

39. Master of Flémalle: *The Holy Trinity*. Frankfurt, Staedel Institute

40. MASTER OF FLÉMALLE: *A Man*. London, National Gallery

41. MASTER OF FLÉMALLE: *A Woman*. London, National Gallery

42. Master of Flémalle: *St. John the Baptist and Heinrich Werl*. Madrid, Prado

43. Master of Flémalle: *St. Barbara*. Madrid, Prado

45. Jaques Daret: *The Visitation, with a Donor.*
Berlin-Dahlem, Staatliche Museen

44. Jaques Daret: *The Adoration of the Kings.*
Berlin-Dahlem, Staatliche Museen

46. Rogier van der Weyden: *The Visitation and a Donor*. Turin, Pinacoteca

47. Rogier van der Weyden: *The Visitation*. Leipzig, Museum

48. Rogier van der Weyden: *Virgin and Child; St. Catherine.* Vienna, Kunsthistorisches Museum

49. ROGIER VAN DER WEYDEN (workshop replica): *The Holy Family; The Lamentation over Christ; Christ appearing to His Mother.* Known as the Miraflores altarpiece. Berlin-Dahlem, Staatliche Museen

50. ROGIER VAN DER WEYDEN: *Christ appearing to His Mother*. New York, Metropolitan Museum of Art

MARIA ERGO ACCEPIT LIBRAM VNGENTI NARDI PISTICI PRETIOSE ET VNXIT PEDES IHV

51. ROGIER VAN DER WEYDEN: *St. Mary Magdalen.* Wing of the Braque triptych. Paris, Louvre

52. Rogier van der Weyden: *The Crucifixion, with Donors; St. Mary Magdalen; St. Veronica.* Vienna, Kunsthistorisches Museum

53. Rogier van der Weyden: *The Descent from the Cross*. Madrid, Prado

54. *The Virgin*. Detail from plate 53

55. *Nicodemus*. Detail from plate 53

56. Rogier van der Weyden: *The Entombment*. Florence, Uffizi

57. ROGIER VAN DER WEYDEN: *Virgin and Child with Saints Peter, John the Baptist, Cosmas and Damian.*
Frankfurt, Staedel Institute

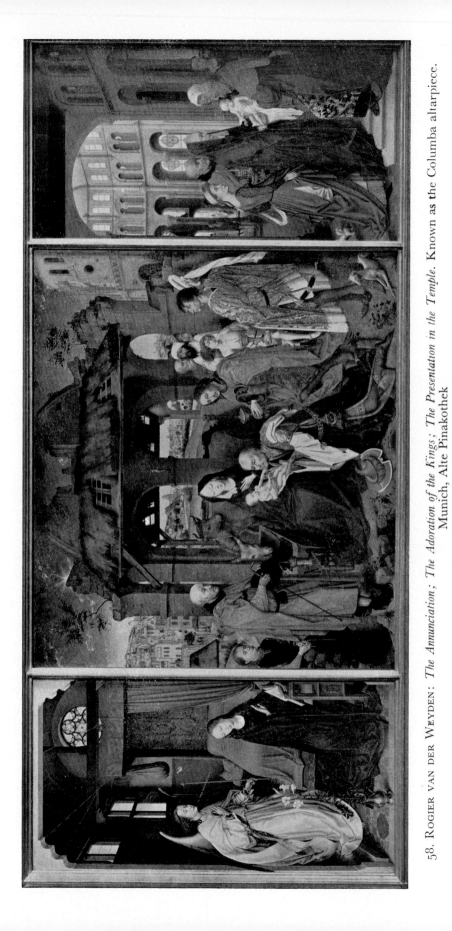

58. Rogier van der Weyden: *The Annunciation; The Adoration of the Kings; The Presentation in the Temple.* Known as the Columba altarpiece. Munich, Alte Pinakothek

59. ROGIER VAN DER WEYDEN: *Virgin and Child appearing to the Emperor Augustus and the Tiburtine Sibyl; The Nativity with the Donor Peeter Bladelin; The Star of Bethlehem appearing to the Kings*. Berlin-Dahlem, Staatliche Museen

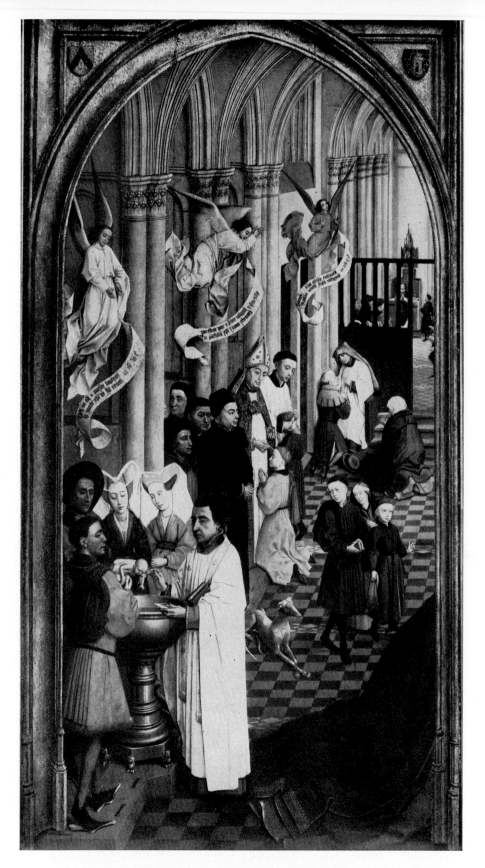

60. ROGIER VAN DER WEYDEN: *Baptism, Confirmation and Confession.*
From the altarpiece of the Sacraments. Antwerp, Museum

61. ROGIER VAN DER WEYDEN: *Marriage, Ordination and Extreme Unction.*
From the altarpiece of the Sacraments. Antwerp, Museum

62. Rogier van der Weyden: *The Last Judgement*. Beaune, Hôtel-Dieu

63. *Damned Souls.* Detail from plate 62

64. *The Last Judgement*. Detail from plate 62

65. ROGIER VAN DER WEYDEN: *St. Luke painting the Virgin*. Boston, Museum of Fine Arts

66. ROGIER VAN DER WEYDEN: *Virgin and Child*. Caen, Museum

67. ROGIER VAN DER WEYDEN: *Laurent Froimont*. Brussels, Museum

68. ROGIER VAN DER WEYDEN: *A Young Woman*. Berlin-Dahlem, Staatliche Museen

69. ROGIER VAN DER WEYDEN: *A Lady*. Washington, National Gallery of Art (Mellon Collection)

70. ROGIER VAN DER WEYDEN: *Philippe de Croy*. Antwerp, Museum

71. Rogier van der Weyden: *Antoine, Grand Bâtard de Bourgogne*. Brussels, Museum

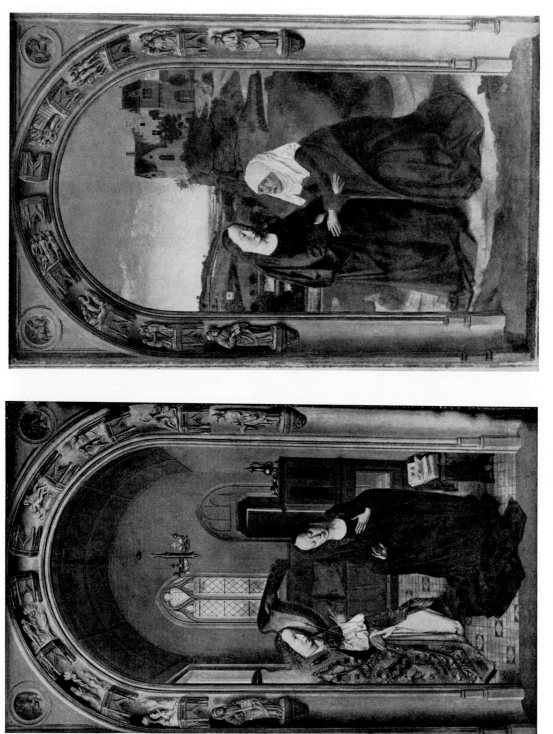

72. Dieric Bouts: *The Annunciation*. Madrid, Prado

73. Dieric Bouts: *The Visitation*. Madrid, Prado

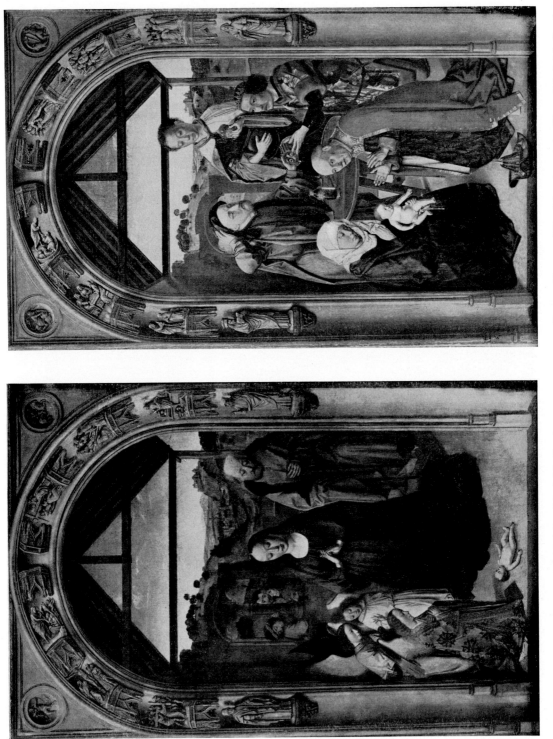

75. DIERIC BOUTS: *The Adoration of the Kings*. Madrid, Prado

74. DIERIC BOUTS: *The Nativity*. Madrid, Prado

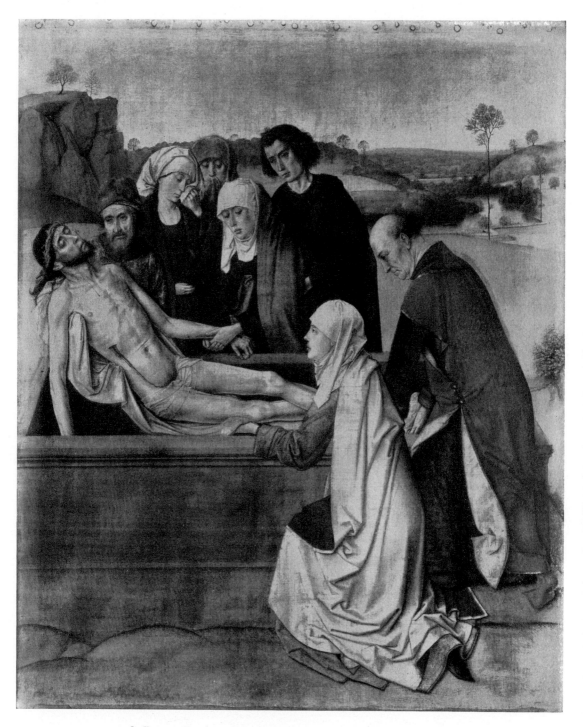

76. Dieric Bouts: *The Entombment.* London, National Gallery

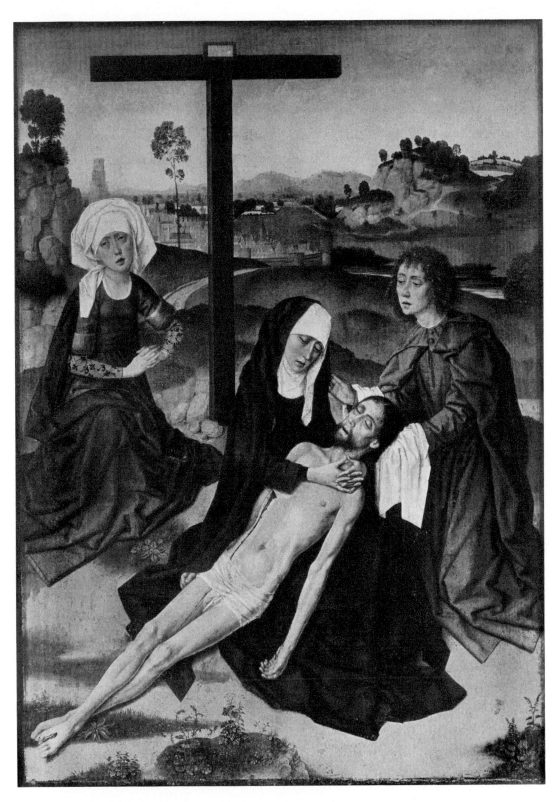

77. Dieric Bouts: *The Lamentation over Christ*. Paris, Louvre

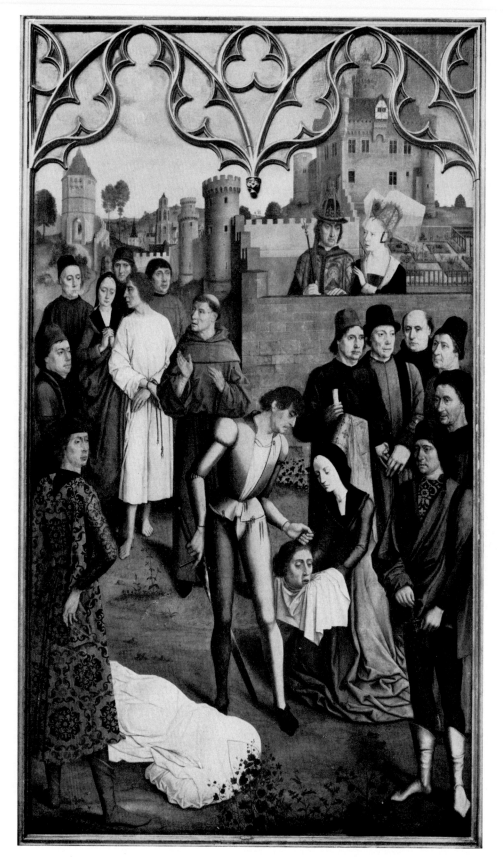

78. DIERIC BOUTS: *The Justice of Emperor Otto*. Brussels, Museum

79. DIERIC BOUTS: *The Justice of Emperor Otto*. Brussels, Museum

80. DIERIC BOUTS: *St. John the Baptist; The Adoration of the Kings; St. Christopher*. Altarpiece known as the 'Pearl of Brabant'. Munich, Alte Pinakothek

81. Dieric Bouts: *The Altarpiece of the Sacrament. Louvain, S. Pierre*

82. DIERIC BOUTS: *Virgin and Child*. London, National Gallery

83. DIERIC BOUTS: *A Man*. London, National Gallery

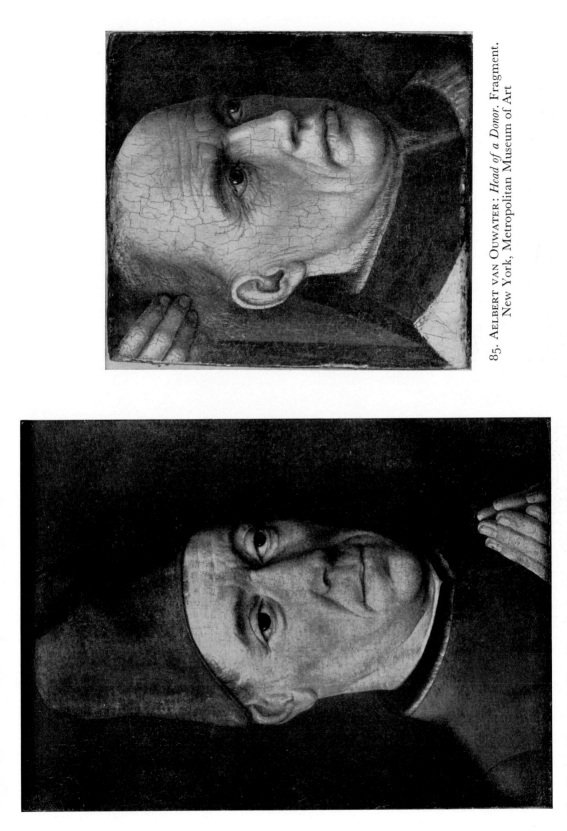

85. Aelbert van Ouwater: *Head of a Donor.* Fragment. New York, Metropolitan Museum of Art

84. Dieric Bouts: *A Man.* New York, Metropolitan Museum of Art

86. AELBERT VAN OUWATER: *The Raising of Lazarus*. Berlin-Dahlem, Staatliche Museen

87. Hugo van der Goes: *Virgin and Child*. Centre panel of a triptych. Frankfurt, Staedel Institute

88. Hugo van der Goes: *The Adoration of the Shepherds.* Centre panel of the Portinari altarpiece. Florence, Uffizi

89. *The Three Kings on the Way to Bethlehem.* Detail from plate 91

90. Hugo van der Goes: *Tommaso Portinari with his Sons and Saints Anthony and Thomas.*
Left wing of the Portinari altarpiece. Florence, Uffizi

91. Hugo van der Goes: *Maria Portinari with her Daughter and Saints Margaret and Mary Magdalen.*
Right wing of the Portinari altarpiece. Florence, Uffizi

92. *Landscape*. Detail from plate 91

93. *The Shepherds*. Detail from plate 88

94. HUGO VAN DER GOES: *The Fall of Man*. Vienna, Kunsthistorisches Museum

95. Hugo van der Goes: *The Lamentation over Christ*. Vienna, Kunsthistorisches Museum

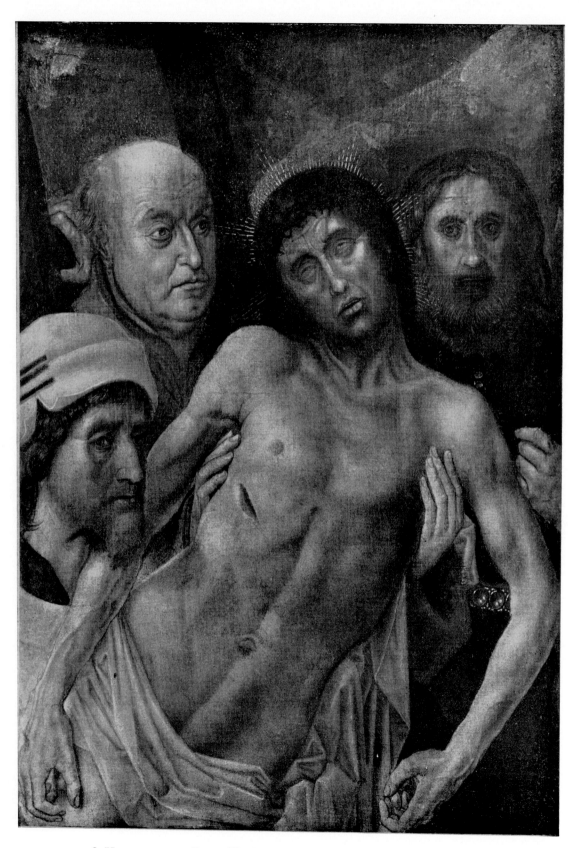

96. Hugo van der Goes: *The Descent from the Cross*. Paris, Wildenstein & Co.

97. HUGO VAN DER GOES: *The Holy Women*. Berlin-Dahlem, Staatliche Museen

98. Hugo van der Goes: *The Adoration of the Shepherds*. Berlin-Dahlem, Staatliche Museen

99. Hugo van der Goes: *The Adoration of the Kings*, Known as the Monforte altarpiece. Berlin-Dahlem, Staatliche Museen

100. HUGO VAN DER GOES: *Sir Edward Bonkil and two Angels*. Edinburgh, National Gallery of Scotland.
On loan from Palace of Holyroodhouse.
Reproduced by gracious permission of Her Majesty The Queen

101. HUGO VAN DER GOES: *The Death of the Virgin*. Bruges, Museum

103. Hugo van der Goes: *Maria Portinari*. Detail from plate 91

102. Hugo van der Goes: *A Man*. New York, Metropolitan Museum of Art

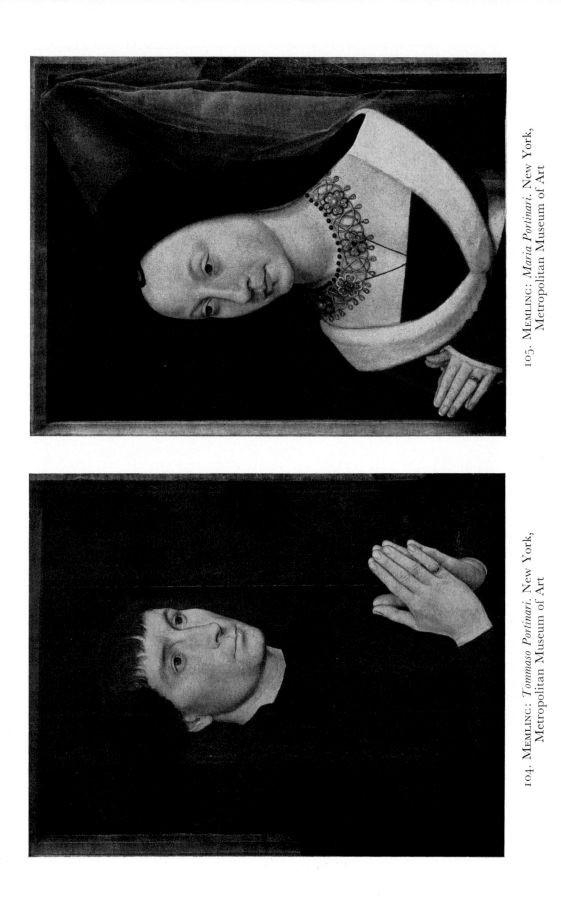

104. MEMLINC: *Tommaso Portinari*. New York,
Metropolitan Museum of Art

105. MEMLINC: *Maria Portinari*. New York,
Metropolitan Museum of Art

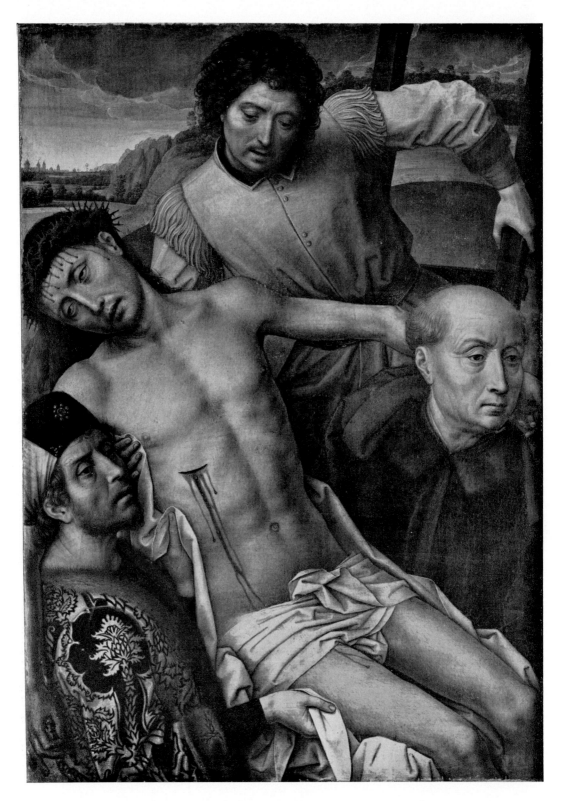

106. MEMLINC: *The Descent from the Cross*. Granada, Capilla Real

107. MEMLINC: *The Holy Women*. Granada, Capilla Real

108. MEMLINC: *Pietà*. Granada, Capilla Real

109. MEMLING: *St. John on Patmos contemplating the Apocalyptic Vision.*
Bruges, Memlinc Museum, St. John's Hospital

110. MEMLINC: *Virgin and Child with Angels, Saints and Donors*. Centre panel of the 'Donne Triptych'. London, National Gallery

111. MEMLINC: *St. John the Baptist and St. John the Evangelist.* Wings of the 'Donne Triptych'.
London, National Gallery

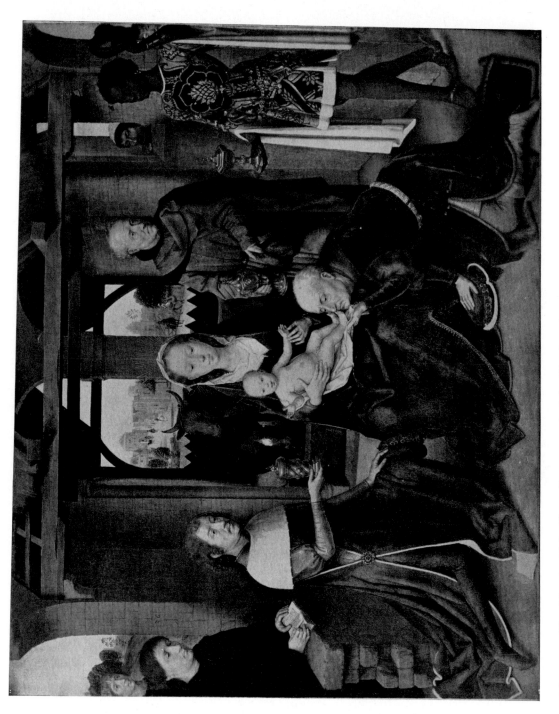

112. MEMLINC:: *The Adoration of the Kings.* Centre panel of the Floreins altarpiece. Bruges, Memlinc Museum, St. John's Hospital

113. MEMLINC: *The Passion of Christ.* Turin, Pinacoteca

114. MEMLINC: *The Martyrdom of St. Ursula's Companions*. From the Shrine of St. Ursula.
Bruges, Memlinc Museum, St. John's Hospital

115. MEMLINC: *The Death of St. Ursula*. From the Shrine of St. Ursula.
Bruges, Memlinc Museum, St. John's Hospital

116. MEMLING: *St. Ursula in Glory with eleven Virgins*. From the Shrine of St. Ursula. Bruges, Memlinc Museum, St. John's Hospital

117. MEMLINC: *St. Ursula sheltering ten Virgins.* From the Shrine of St. Ursula.
Bruges, Memlinc Museum, St. John's Hospital

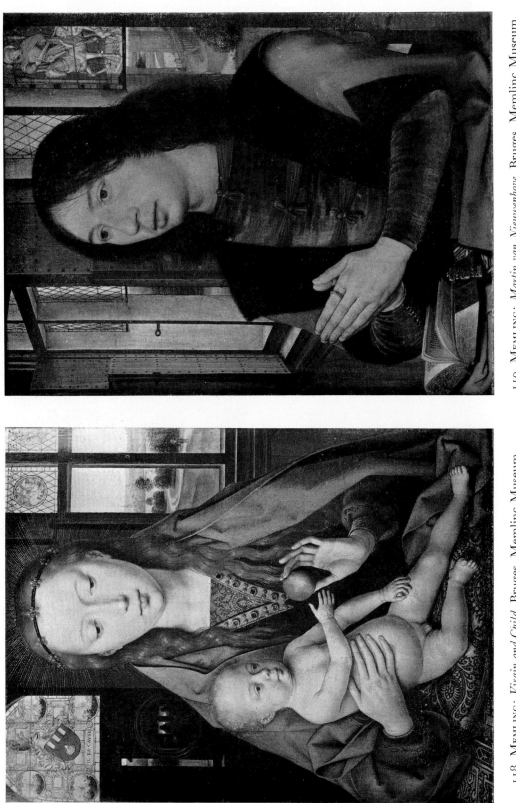

118. MEMLINC: *Virgin and Child.* Bruges, Memlinc Museum,
St. John's Hospital

119. MEMLINC: *Martin van Nieuwenhove.* Bruges, Memlinc Museum,
St. John's Hospital

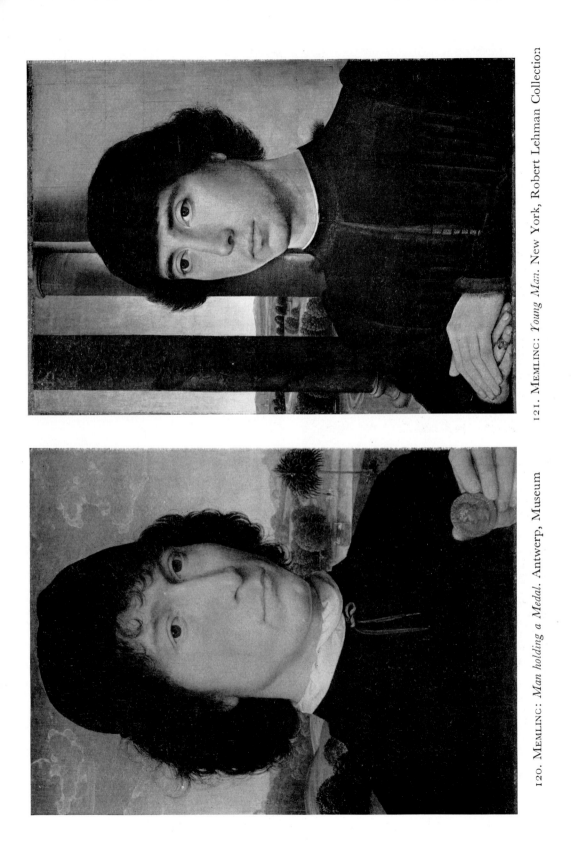

120. Memlinc: *Man holding a Medal*. Antwerp, Museum

121. Memlinc: *Young Man*. New York, Robert Lehman Collection

122. MEMLINC: *Lady with a Pink*. New York,
Metropolitan Museum of Art

123. MEMLINC: *Two Horses*. Rotterdam,
Museum Boymans-van Beuningen

124. MEMLINC: *Maria Moreel*. Bruges, Memlinc Museum, St. John's Hospital

125. GERARD DAVID: *Canon de Salviatis with Saints Donatian, Bernardino and Martin.*
London, National Gallery

126. GERARD DAVID: *The Verdict of Cambyses*. Bruges, Museum

127. GERARD DAVID: *Virgin and Child with Angels and female Saints*. Rouen, Museum

128. GERARD DAVID: *The Marriage of Cana, with the Donor Jean de Sedano and his Family*. Paris, Louvre

129. GERARD DAVID: *Virgin and Child*. Von Pannwitz Collection

130. GERARD DAVID: *Two Landscapes*. Amsterdam, Rijksmuseum

131. GERARD DAVID: *The Baptism of Christ. Bruges, Museum; on the wings: The Donor, Jan de Trompes and his Son with St. John the Evangelist; the Donor's first Wife and their Daughters with St. Elizabeth*

132. GERARD DAVID: *Virgin and Child with Saints Barbara, Mary Magdalen, Catherine and the Donor Richardus de Capella*. London, National Gallery

133. Master of the Virgo inter Virgines: *The Annunciation*. Rotterdam, Museum Boymans-van Beuningen

134. Justus van Gent: *The Last Supper*. Urbino, Palazzo Ducale

135. JUSTUS VAN GENT: *The Crucifixion*. Ghent, St. Bavo

136. GEERTGEN TOT SINT JANS: *The Raising of Lazarus*. Paris, Louvre

137. GEERTGEN TOT SINT JANS: *The Burning of the Bones of St. John.* Vienna, Kunsthistorisches Museum

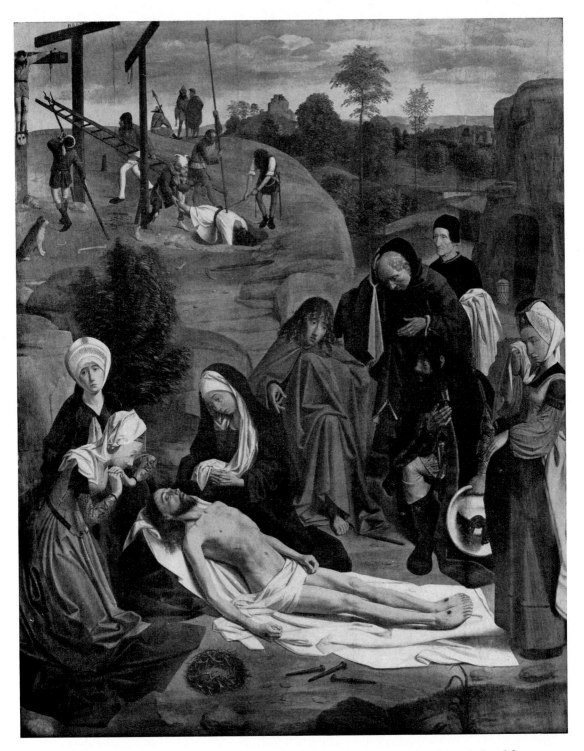

138. GEERTGEN TOT SINT JANS: *The Lamentation over Christ*. Vienna, Kunsthistorisches Museum

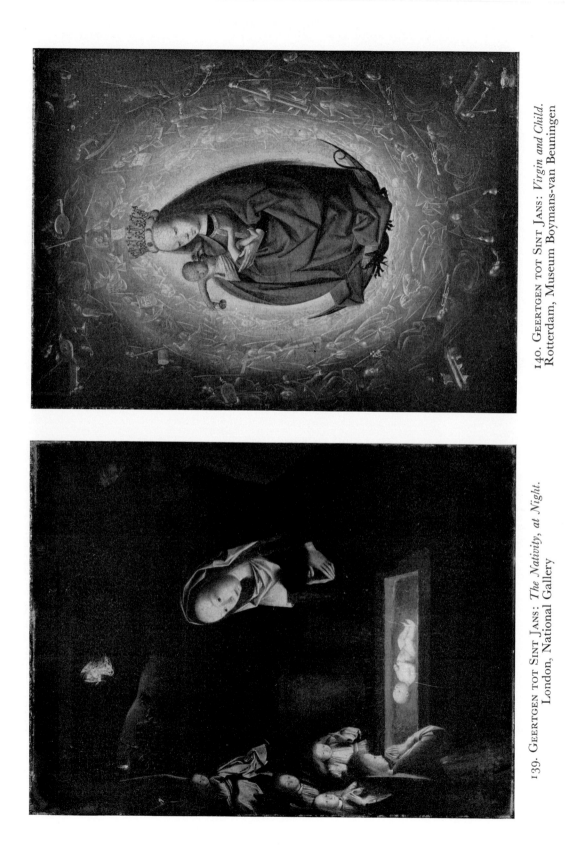

140. Geertgen tot Sint Jans: *Virgin and Child.*
Rotterdam, Museum Boymans-van Beuningen

139. Geertgen tot Sint Jans: *The Nativity, at Night.*
London, National Gallery

141. GEERTGEN TOT SINT JANS: *The Adoration of the Kings.* Cleveland, Museum of Art (Gift of Hanna Fund)

142. GEERTGEN TOT SINT JANS: *St. John the Baptist in the Wilderness.* Berlin-Dahlem, Staatliche Museen

143. GEERTGEN TOT SINT JANS: *Christ as Man of Sorrows*. Utrecht, Archiepiscopal Museum

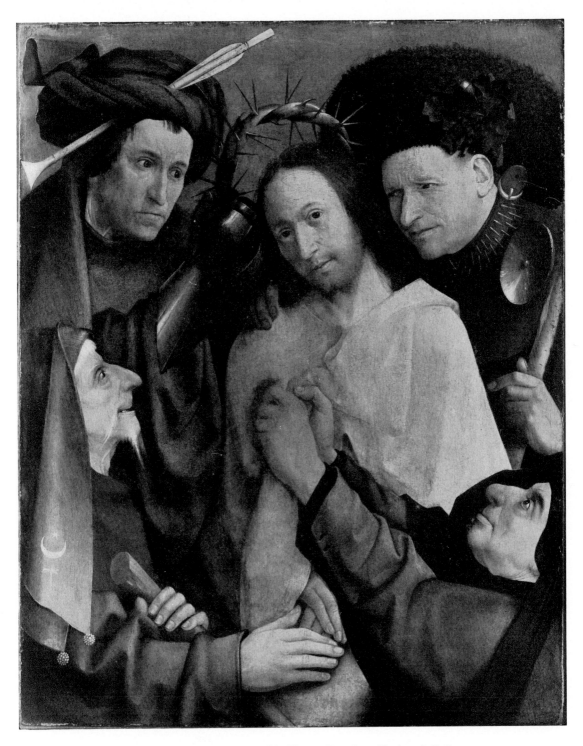

144. BOSCH: *The Crowning with Thorns*. London, National Gallery

145. BOSCH: *Table top with the Seven Deadly Sins*. Madrid, Prado

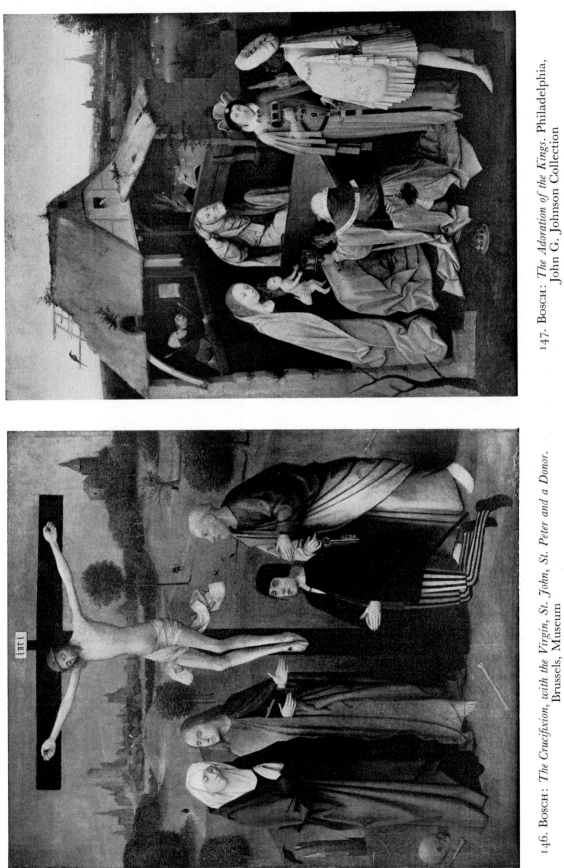

146. Bosch: *The Crucifixion, with the Virgin, St. John, St. Peter and a Donor.* Brussels, Museum

147. Bosch: *The Adoration of the Kings.* Philadelphia, John G. Johnson Collection

148–149. Bosch: *St. Peter with a Donor; St. Agnes with the Donor's Wife.* Wings of plate 150.
Madrid, Prado

150. BOSCH: *The Adoration of the Kings*. Madrid, Prado

151. BOSCH: *The Garden of Earthly Delights*. Centre panel of a triptych. Madrid, Prado

152. BOSCH: *The Hay-Wain*. Centre panel of a triptych. Escorial

153. BOSCH: *The Temptation of St. Anthony.* Lisbon, Museum

154. BOSCH: *St. Jerome in Penitence*. Ghent, Museum

155. Bosch: *Ecce homo*. Philadelphia, John G. Johnson Collection

156. Bosch: *Christ carrying the Cross*. Ghent, Museum

157. BOSCH: *The Mocking of Christ*. Escorial

158. BOSCH: *The Prodigal Son*. Rotterdam,
Museum Boymans-van Beuningen

159. Bosch: *St. John on Patmos*. Berlin-Dahlem, Staatliche Museen

LIST OF PLATES
INDEX OF PLACES

ACKNOWLEDGEMENTS

Plate 100 is reproduced by gracious permission of Her Majesty the Queen.

We wish to express our sincere gratitude to the following private owners and museum authorities for permission to reproduce paintings in their collections and for supplying photographs:

The late Mr. D. G. van Beuningen; Mr. Robert Lehman; Mme von Pannwitz; the Earl of Verulam.

Rijksmuseum, Amsterdam; Musée Royal, Antwerp; Staatliche Museen, Berlin-Dahlem; Museum of Fine Arts, Boston; Memlinc Museum, St. John's Hospital, Bruges; Herzog Anton Ulrich Museum, Brunswick; Devonshire Collection, Chatsworth; Museum of Art, Cleveland; Staedel Institute, Frankfurt; National Gallery, London; Prado, Madrid; Alte Pinakothek, Munich; Metropolitan Museum, New York; Frick Collection, New York; John G. Johnson Art Collection, Philadelphia; Museum Boymans-Van Beuningen, Rotterdam; Kunsthistorisches Museum, Vienna; National Gallery of Art, Washington, D.C.

Further photographs have been supplied by A.C.L., Brussels; De Spaarnestad, Haarlem; Alinari, Florence; Archives Photographiques, Paris; Bulloz, Paris; Giraudon, Paris; and Anderson, Rome.

LIST OF PLATES

COLOUR PLATES

INDEX OF PLACES

INDEX OF PLACES

NEW YORK, Metropolitan Museum
Christus, 28, 31; Master of Flémalle, 33; Rogier, 50; Bouts, 84; Ouwater, 85; Goes, 102; Memlinc, 104, 105, 122

NEW YORK, Frick Collection
Van Eyck, 15

NEW YORK, Robert Lehman Collection
Christus, 32; Memlinc, 121

PARIS, Louvre
Van Eyck, 12; Rogier, 51; Bouts, 77; David, 128; Geertgen, 136

PARIS, Wildenstein & Co.
Goes, 96

PHILADELPHIA, John G. Johnson Art Collection
Van Eyck, 24; Bosch, 147, 155

ROTTERDAM, Museum Boymans-Van Beuningen
Van Eyck, 11; Memlinc, 123; Master of Virgo inter Virgines, 133; Geertgen, 140; Bosch, 158

ROUEN, Museum
David, 127

TURIN, Museo Civico
Book of Hours, 22, (23)

TURIN, Pinacoteca
Rogier, 46; Memlinc, 113

URBINO, Palazzo Ducale
Justus van Gent, 134

UTRECHT, Archiepiscopal Museum
Geertgen, 143

VIENNA, Kunsthistorisches Museum
Van Eyck, 17; Rogier, 48, 52; Goes, 94, 95; Geertgen, 137, 138

WASHINGTON, National Gallery of Art
Van Eyck, 14; Christus, 29; Rogier, 69

Von Pannwitz Collection (formerly)
David, 129